Trouble in Seventh Heaven

Jo Sykes

Compact Verlag

Bisher sind in dieser Reihe erschienen:

Band 1: Full Moon Kisses
Band 2: Last Chance for a First Date
Band 3: Flirt But Don't Fall in Love
Band 4: Trouble in Seventh Heaven

Weitere Titel sind in Vorbereitung.

© 2009 Compact Verlag München
Alle Rechte vorbehalten. Nachdruck, auch auszugsweise, nur mit ausdrücklicher Genehmigung des Verlages gestattet.
Chefredaktion: Dr. Angela Sendlinger
Redaktion: Helga Aichele
Fachredaktion: Yasmin und Richard Robinson
Produktion: Wolfram Friedrich
Illustrationen: Bettina Weisl (MA Illustration)
Typografischer Entwurf: textum GmbH
Umschlaggestaltung: Bettina Weisl (MA Illustration)

ISBN: 978-3-8174-7826-2
7278261

Besuche uns im Internet: www.compactverlag.de

Vorwort

Mit dieser spannenden und romantischen Compact Lovestory kannst du deine Englischkenntnisse spielend leicht verbessern. Eine deutsche Einleitung vor jedem neuen Kapitel hilft dir, den englischen Text zu verstehen. Außerdem werden auf jeder Seite die etwas schwierigeren Wörter erklärt, und durch die Zeichnungen bekommst du eine genauere Vorstellung von den vier Girls und ihren aufregenden Erlebnissen. Blätter doch einfach mal durch!

Jedes Kapitel wird durch Übungen und Tests ergänzt, die richtig spannend und abwechslungsreich sind: Da geht es um Jungs und Liebe, Partys, Freundschaft und Mode – so wird Englisch lernen richtig spannend und cool!

Die Antworten und Lösungen kannst du gleich ins Buch schreiben und hinterher im Lösungsteil nachlesen, ob du alles richtig gemacht hast und was die Tests über dich aussagen. Und wenn du möchtest, kannst du alle Vokabeln im Glossar noch einmal nachschlagen. Slang-Ausdrücke sind mit einem ⚡ gekennzeichnet.

Wir wünschen dir viel Spaß mit Emily und ihren Freundinnen – und natürlich viel Erfolg beim Englisch lernen!

Inhalt

Kapitel 1:	Auditions and Birthdays	5
Kapitel 2:	Monday Morning Trouble	25
Kapitel 3:	There's Trouble in Seventh Heaven	47
Kapitel 4:	Secrets and Milkshakes	67
Kapitel 5:	True Colours and True Crushes	91
Lösungen		113
Glossar		120

Auditions and Birthdays

1

Emily möchte im Schultheaterstück *Seventh Heaven* die weibliche Hauptrolle „Jenny" spielen, denn ihr Schwarm Michael hat für die männliche Hauptrolle des Stücks vorgesprochen. Emily träumt davon, gemeinsam mit Michael auf der Bühne zu stehen. Dann könnte sie ihm als Jenny ihre Gefühle gestehen! Hoffentlich macht ihr Andrew, ihr etwas langweiliger Nachbar, nicht einen Strich durch die Rechnung, denn auch er will die Hauptrolle spielen.
Emily ist so in ihre Tagträume vertieft, dass sie noch schusseliger ist als sonst. Das bleibt nicht ohne Folgen …

Please, Reece! I love you, Reece! I love you more than anyone in the whole world, and I can't imagine my life without you. I'm so sorry for what I've done, and I promise that I'll never ever hurt you again. I won't stop loving you –

Of course these were not Emily's own thoughts; they were Jenny's words. "Jenny" was the main female character in the school play *Seventh Heaven*. It was a Friday afternoon and Emily was walking home from an audition for the part of Jenny in the play. Now she was thinking about Jenny's lines. Hopefully I'll have the opportunity to say these lines again, she thought.

Emily thought Jenny was a brilliant character. Jenny seemed like everything Emily wanted to be: confident, daring, independent and, most of all, in love.

Emily enjoyed drama. But she had auditioned for the play for another reason: Emily wanted to prove to herself and to her friends that she, too, could be a leader. She wanted to show her classmates that she could be confident, daring and independent, just like Jenny. And of course, most importantly, Emily wanted to show the world that, just like Jenny in the play, she was in love... in love with Michael Fernandez.

main female character	weibliche Hauptfigur
school play	Schultheaterstück
audition	Vorsprechen
part	Rolle
confident	sebstbewusst
daring	wagemutig
to audition	vorsprechen
to prove	beweisen
stunningly	erstaunlich
root	Wurzel
smooth	glatt, weich
spot	Pickel

Michael Fernandez. He was as exotic as his name, stunningly attractive and full of romance. Michael Fernandez. He was the boy with Spanish roots and wonderful olive-brown, soft, smooth and clear skin. The majority of teenagers of Emily's age had faces covered in spots – it sadly was a part of being a teenager for everyone... for everyone except Michael.

Michael styled his straight, dark hair every morning before school, so that it looked amazing all day long.

He had all the coolest things: a fantastic mobile phone, a modern MP3 player and even an expensive watch. When he did not have to wear his school uniform, Michael wore trendy designer clothes from the nicest shops.

Although Emily liked all of these things, something else about Michael Fernandez was much more special.

Emily loved Michael's smile. In fact, Emily was in love with Michael's smile.

Above all, Emily had auditioned for the part of Jenny for this reason: Michael had auditioned for the part of "Reece" (the main male part in the play – Jenny's boyfriend).

I will be Jenny and Michael will be Reece, thought Emily, and my dream of being Michael's true girlfriend will be one step closer to reality...

"Emily!" cried a voice from down the street. It was waking Emily up from her daydream. "Wait for me!"

It was Andrew Howard. Andrew was Emily's next-door neighbour. He and Emily walked to school together every morning and often walked home from school in the evening. He was a nice boy, and Emily enjoyed being his friend. Some people at school thought Andrew was un-cool because he did not have expensive trendy clothes, and he did not play football.

amazing	super, erstaunlich
daydream	Tagtraum

straight = glatt / gerade
even = sogar
although = obwohl
something else =
above all = vor allem

Andrew knew that, but he didn't mind. He was happy wearing his baggy jeans, instead of the newest, trendy ones. And he was happy listening to rock bands and playing the guitar while the other boys played football.

Emily waited for Andrew. She was slightly confused. Why was Andrew walking home from school now, so late? Emily herself was so late because she had been at the audition. But where had Andrew been?

"How was the audition?" asked Andrew.

"Fine, thanks," replied Emily. "I think it went well. Where have you been? Why are you only going home now?"

ÜBUNG 1: Match-up. *Verbinde die folgenden Verben mit ihrer Ergänzung!*

1. to play — the guitar
2. to audition — for a play
3. to wear — trendy designer clothes
4. to love — somebody's smile
5. to walk — to school
6. to listen — to rock bands
7. to style — your hair

"Well," said Andrew, "guess what... I auditioned, too. For the part of Reece!"

"Really!" said Emily, in a surprised voice. "That's a surprise. I didn't see you, and besides, I thought the auditions for the part of Reece were yesterday?"

"Yes, they were," replied Andrew, "but yesterday I had my guitar lesson, so I had an audition with Mr Adams today."

"Oh," said Emily. She was slightly disappointed [enttäuscht] and a little annoyed, too. Andrew was a good actor. A very good actor. Maybe better than Michael. If Emily got the part of Jenny, but Andrew, not Michael, got the part of Reece, it would be a disaster!

"How was your audition?" she asked, trying [versuchen] not to seem disappointed.

He didn't mind.	Es war ihm egal.
baggy	schlabberig, sackartig
slightly confused	ein bisschen verwirrt
to reply	antworten
besides	außerdem
annoyed	verärgert
actor	Schauspieler
↯ to have a crush on sb.	in jmd. verknallt sein

"Okay, I think," said Andrew, "but tell me more about yours. How many girls auditioned for Jenny?"

"Four," said Emily. "Firstly there was Nina. She really wants the part because she has a crush on Michael Fernandez, who also [auch] auditioned for Reece."

Nina was one of Emily's best friends. In fact, Emily had three best friends;

Nina, Holly and Evie. Emily and her three best friends were all taking part in the play in some way, either on stage, acting, or backstage, designing costumes and the set. The four girls talked about almost everything together: boys, clothes, school and the rest. Nina had a huge crush on Michael; that was a fact. She wrote "Nina loves Michael" on her pencil case. Emily did not speak German very well, but she understood "Ich liebe Michael" perfectly, because Nina wrote it all over her schoolbooks!

But almost everything is not the same as everything. Emily, of course, also had a crush on Michael, something that she never told her friends because she was scared that Nina would be angry. For a while Emily had gone out with a boy called Nathan. But eventually they split up and, within a couple of weeks, Michael started going to Emily's school. Emily soon fell for the new boy, but this time Nina fell for the same boy.

"Secondly, there was Samantha Lavigne," continued Emily. "She was rubbish. I know she plays the clarinet well, but she certainly can't act! She just wants to be famous. She

backstage	hinter der Bühne
huge	riesig
to go out with sb.	mit jmd. (aus)gehen
to split up	(sich) trennen
to fall for sb.	sich in jmd. verknallen
⚡ She was rubbish.	Sie war grottenschlecht.
certainly	zweifellos

[handwritten at top: either … or … = entweder … oder / of course = natürlich]

thinks she's so amazing at everything, but really she's nothing more than an attention-seeker."

"I can imagine that," said Andrew. "She's unfriendly and selfish – she seems to think about nobody but herself. I really hope she doesn't get the part."

"Yeah, I agree," said Emily. "Thirdly, there was Laura Padbury. She's a very good actress... but so nervous and shy! She needs more confidence."

"I had no idea she liked acting," said Andrew. "Every day I see her on her own, without any friends. I really don't think I have ever spoken to her. She's so quiet."

They continued walking together, past the newsagent's, the butcher's and the bakery, up the hill and along their street until they were home.

"Well, have a nice weekend, Andrew," said Emily, as she walked up to her front door.

attention-seeker	jmd., der die Beachtung von anderen sucht
selfish	egoistisch
actress	Schauspielerin
shy	schüchtern
newsagent's	Zeitungskiosk
awkwardly	ungeschickt
ice-cream parlour	Eisdiele

"Errrm, yeah, thanks," replied Andrew awkwardly.

He really wanted to ask Emily if she wanted to do something at the weekend: go to the cinema, go for a walk or even just go to the ice-cream parlour together. However, Andrew was too nervous to ask her. Emily spent all of her free time with Nina, Holly and Evie – why would she want to spend time with him?

ÜBUNG 2: True or false? Korrigiere die falschen Sätze!

1. Emily did not know why Andrew was walking home so late.

   ....~~dasaorld~~...

2. Emily thought the auditions for the part of Reece were the following day.

   ....

3. Emily was scared that Andrew might be a better actor than Michael.

   ....

4. Emily didn't understand when Nina wrote „Ich liebe Michael" on her pencil case.

   ....

5. Samantha has more acting ability than Laura.

   ....

to pluck up the courage to do sth.	sich ein Herz fassen, etw. zu tun
to appear	erscheinen
to get on with sb.	mit jmd. auskommen

Emily smiled at him, and then, just as she opened the door, Andrew plucked up the courage to ask Emily the question.

"What... errrm... are you, errrm... doing tomorrow, Emily?" Andrew was bright red.

Emily stopped and began to think. What was she doing tomorrow? She was sure she had something planned. What was it? She couldn't remember. Surely it was nothing important.

I don't think I'm doing anything, Andrew," Emily replied with a small smile. "Why?"

"Oh... errrrm... so do you want to..." began Andrew. But then Mrs Etchells, Emily's mother, appeared at the door.

"Emily's coming shopping with me!" said Mrs Etchells. "What do you think, Emily? Mother and daughter, girly day at the shops?"

"Great!" said Emily. "See you later, Andrew!"

"Oh... okay... see you on..." began Andrew, but before he could finish Emily had already gone into her house and shut the door.

The next day was Saturday, and Mrs Etchells and Emily went to town shopping together.

Emily enjoyed spending time with her mother. In general, Emily got on well with her parents. Of course, they were strict and had some serious rules. For example, Emily had to finish her homework before she saw Holly, Evie and Nina. And when Emily stayed at a friend's house, Mr or Mrs Etchells always telephoned to check that her friend's parents were at home. However, Emily did not mind. She knew that her parents had rules because they loved her.

"Do you like those brown shoes?" said Mrs Etchells when they walked past *Hodge's Shoes*, a very posh shoe shop in town. It was nearly seven o'clock, and they had been shopping for hours.

"No!" cried Emily. "They're awful! They're too old-fashioned. I like the red ones. They're really pretty."

posh = piekfein

"Pretty?!" said Mrs Etchells, and laughed. "They are ugly!"

"No way!" cried Emily. "They're gorgeous! And I'll prove it to you. I'll take a picture of them with my camera-phone and show Nina. She's a fashion queen, isn't she? And I'm sure she'll think they are gorgeous. So if Nina says they are gorgeous, they're officially gorgeous."

Mrs Etchells laughed. "Okay, do it. It's true, Nina is very stylish, and if she likes them, I will accept that I am old and out of touch with today's trends!"

strict	streng
No way!	Auf keinen Fall!
gorgeous	wunderschön, großartig
stylish	modisch, stylish
annoying	ärgerlich
never mind	macht nichts, mach dir nichts daraus

Emily put her hand in her pocket to take out her phone... but it was not there.

"Oh no!" muttered Emily. "I've left my mobile at home! How annoying!"

"Never mind," said Mrs Etchells, "you can show Nina next time you are both in town."

"Yes, I suppose so," replied Emily.

As they continued shopping together, Emily thought about the play, *Seventh Heaven*. I wonder who will get the part of Jenny? Maybe Laura, so quiet, but an amazing actress? Or

Samantha, such an awful actress, but so ambitious? Maybe it'll be Nina. She would be so happy! And I want her to be happy. But I don't want to imagine Nina acting alongside Michael. ... It would be impossible not to feel jealous. I love Michael so much!

But I mustn't forget that my friends are more important than a play. Nina, Holly, Evie and I will always be friends –

the play isn't going to change that.

"Emily... Emily?... Emily!" said Mrs Etchells in a loud voice. "Are you day-dreaming again? Do you want to go into the card shop? It's your dad's birthday next week. Do you want to buy him a card now?"

ambitious	ehrgeizig
jealous	eifersüchtig
to realize	bemerken, begreifen

Of course, thought Emily. Dad's birthday. Next week. But wait, someone else's birthday came before then. Suddenly Emily remembered.

"Oh no!" she cried. "No! I can't believe it! I've forgotten Evie's birthday... today! Oh, Mum! I'm an awful friend. How could I forget? Now I remember my original plan for today. I was supposed to go for lunch with Holly, Nina and, of course, Evie. Then we planned to go to the cinema together. It's Evie's special day, and I forgot. I'm so stupid. How will she ever forgive me, Mum? She's one of my very best friends."

"Oh Emily... I knew you were forgetful, but I didn't realize you were so forgetful. But don't worry," said Mrs Etchells calmly. "I'm sure she will understand because she is one of your best friends. Now come on, let's buy your dad a birthday card before the shop shuts!"

When they arrived home, Emily ran upstairs to find her mobile phone, which she had left behind earlier in the day.

ÜBUNG 3: Unscramble the text! Ordne die folgenden Sätze chronologisch.

a) Mrs Etchells asks Emily for her opinion on a pair of brown shoes in *Hodges Shoes*.

b) Andrew asks Emily what she is doing the next day.

c) Mrs Etchells agrees that Nina is very trendy.

d) Emily realizes she has left her phone at home.

e) Emily wishes Andrew a good weekend.

f) Mrs Etchells asks Emily if she'd like to go shopping the next day.

g) Emily says she prefers the red shoes to the brown ones.

1	2	3	4	5	6	7
e						

She had received four text messages:
First new message. From NINA at 14.06:

> hi emily! where r u? r u late? we arranged 2 meet @ sankeys cafe @ 2 4 evies bday lunch, remember? come kwikly. luv nina x x x

Second new message. From HOLLY at 14.12:

> hurry up emily. wher r u. wer in sankeys now. wanna order food. c u soon. Luv holly x x

Third new message. From HOLLY at 14.34:

> emily this isnt funny. wher r u? evies worried uv 4gotten. plz txt bk. u still comin 2 cinema? film starts @ 4 – plz come, holly x

Forth new message. From NINA at 15.54:

> hi Emily, plz txt bk!! wer goin in2 cinema now. u need 2 spk 2 evie 2 xplain everything cos shes rly upset. hope u r ok. is ther a prob? Luv nina xx

Emily felt awful. She tried to ring Evie. And she tried again. And again. And again. But nobody answered. She began to write a text message to Evie, but she was interrupted by Mrs Etchells calling her.

"Emily! Come downstairs! There's a message for you on the answer-phone from Miss Moss!"

Miss Moss was the co-director of the school play. Maybe it was news about the audition? Emily ran downstairs, into the kitchen, and pressed play on the answer-phone. This is what she heard:

text message	SMS
to arrange to meet	sich verabreden
answer-phone	Anrufbeantworter
co-director	Mitregisseurin
sensation	Gefühl
guilt	Schuld

"Hello. This is a message for Emily. It's Miss Moss from school. I'm pleased to offer you the part of Jenny. I hope you'll accept it. Michael Fernandez has already accepted the part of Reece. Let me know on Monday, okay? Enjoy the rest of your weekend. Bye!"

Wow! Emily was shocked. This was brilliant. But instead of feeling happy, Emily felt a strange sensation of enormous guilt. How could she be happy when she had forgotten her best friend's birthday?

ÜBUNG 4: Text messaging. Verwende die SMS von Nina und Holly, um die folgenden Wörter und Ausdrücke in die „SMS-Sprache" zu übersetzen!

1. are   r
2. kiss   x
3. please   pl2
4. really   ....
5. see you soon ....
6. birthday   b-day
7. text back   ....
8. for   ....
9. problem   ....
10. to   ....
11. love   luv
12. we are   ....

Emily sighed. "I'm so stupid, Mum," she said. "Evie must hate me."

"Evie does not hate you," answered Mrs Etchells reassuringly. "She just must be a bit upset. Go and send her a text message now, so at least she knows you haven't forgotten completely. I'm sure she'll be fine on Monday."

"Okay, maybe you're right, Mum," answered Emily, sadly. However, in reality, this was just the beginning of the serious trouble in seventh heaven to come.

to sigh	seufzen
reassuringly	beruhigend

Monday Morning Trouble

2

Toll, Emily wird Jenny spielen! Aber anstatt sich zu freuen, hat sie ein total schlechtes Gewissen Evie gegenüber. Emily will sich entschuldigen, doch Evie ignoriert sie und lässt sie einfach stehen. Wenigstens Nina und Holly freuen sich, dass Emily die Rolle bekommen hat, aber für Emily ist der Tag verkorkst. Die fiesen Bemerkungen der neidischen Schulzicke Samantha heben Emilys Stimmung auch nicht gerade. Und als sie in der Pause dann zu allem Überfluss auch noch einen anonymen Drohbrief in ihrem Spind findet, gibt ihr das den Rest! Haben sich denn alle gegen sie verschworen?

Sunday passed and Monday morning arrived: the beginning of a new week. Monday mornings did not usually bother Emily, because she could see her friends and listen to their stories from the weekend. However, Emily was not looking forward to school on this particular morning. I've messed up the stories from this weekend, she thought, and packed her schoolbooks and pencil case into her school bag.
She put on her shoes and jacket and said goodbye to her mother. Then she went round to Andrew's house and knocked on the

door. Andrew answered the door quickly, as always, and was ready to go to school on time, as always.

"Hey Emily!" said Andrew, smiling. "Congratulations on getting the part of Jenny!"

"Oh, thanks Andrew," replied Emily, "but how did you know?"

"Mr Adams told me. He rang to tell me I'm the understudy for the part of Reece. Isn't it great! I know the actual part would be better, but I'm not bothered. It isn't a surprise that Michael Fernandez got the actual part – I expected him to get it. And if nothing goes wrong, and Michael plays Reece in the performances, I'll be happy with my small part – Mr Neville, the headmaster."

They set off walking to school together. Andrew was so excited about the

to bother	stören
particular	bestimmt
Congratulations!	Glückwunsch!
understudy	Zweitbesetzung
actual	tatsächlich, eigentlich
to expect	erwarten
performance	Aufführung, Darbietung
disinterested	desinteressiert

play that it was all he wanted to talk about. Slowly, however, he realized that Emily was not as enthusiastic.

"Are you okay, Emily?" he asked. "I thought you would be excited about the play, but instead you seem... disinterested. Is something wrong?"

"It's a long story," Emily sighed.

"We've still got a long way to go before we get to school," replied Andrew, "certainly long enough for a long story."

ÜBUNG 5: Multiple choice. Wähle die richtige Fortsetzung zu jedem Satzanfang!

1. Emily isn't looking forward to going to school because...
    a) ❏ she doesn't want to listen to her friends' stories.
    b) ❏ she thinks she has spoilt the weekend's stories.
    c) ❏ her pencil case won't fit in her schoolbag.

2. On the way to school Emily wants to talk about...
    a) ❏ the play.
    b) ❏ Michael Fernandez.
    c) ❏ why she feels sad.

3. Andrew will only play Reece if...
    a) ❏ nothing goes wrong.
    b) ❏ he can't play Mr Neville.
    c) ❏ Michael can't.

4. Andrew thinks that Emily seems...
    a) ❏ far too enthusiastic.
    b) ❏ less interested than he expected.
    c) ❏ deeply upset.

So Emily explained to Andrew why she was feeling down and showed him the text messages from Holly and Nina. "Evie has not replied to any of my text messages or answered any of my phone calls," remarked Emily. "I rang and texted her all day yesterday, too! And now I'm scared of seeing her because I know she's going to be very upset."

Andrew wasn't sure how to react. He wasn't very good at giving advice.

"I'm sure Evie will understand," he said, very unconvincingly, as they arrived at the school gates. What a stupid thing to say, Andrew thought to himself.

to feel down	niedergeschlagen sein
to remark	bemerken, anmerken
to react	reagieren
unconvincingly	wenig überzeugend
to chat	sich unterhalten, plaudern
to apologize	sich entschuldigen

"Thanks Andrew," replied Emily, "but I really don't think it is that simple. Okay... the girls are over there," she said and pointed to Evie, Holly and Nina, who were standing and chatting near the main entrance to the school. "I'll apologize now, face to face. Wish me luck."

This should be interesting, Andrew thought to himself, as Emily walked to where her friends were standing.

"Hi!" Emily shouted. "How is everyone? Listen, I just want to say that I am *so* sorry for..."

But before Emily could finish, Evie turned to Holly and Nina and said, "Oh, I have to

speak to Mrs Phillips before registration. I'll see you at break, okay?"

Emily's heart sank. She was shocked. The situation was even worse than she had expected.

"Hi Emily!" said Holly, brightly. "How are you? Did you have a nice weekend?"

There was a short, awkward moment of silence, then Holly continued, "Look, Evie was really upset on Saturday. Why didn't you come? Was something wrong?"

"I just... forgot," answered Emily. "I don't know how. I don't know why. I'm so sorry! I was just in town with my mum and... it was so nice to spend time with my mum... we had such a nice day together and... I don't know. I'm just so forgetful. And..." Emily paused.

"And what?" asked Nina.

"And I have thought about *Seventh Heaven* so much lately. It has been the only thing on my mind."

"Don't worry, Emily," said Nina. "We know you haven't forgotten about us really. It's clear that you didn't upset Evie on purpose, but you have to show her how sorry you are."

"That's what I'm trying to do!" Emily replied.

registration	Anwesenheitskontrolle
sb.'s heart sinks	jmd. rutscht das Herz in die Hose
to have sth. on one's mind	etw. im Sinn haben
on purpose	mit Absicht
stubborn	stur
understanding	verständnisvoll
to march up to sb.	auf jmd. zumarschieren
tied tightly	fest gebunden

"Yeah, we know," said Nina, "but, you know, Evie can be quite stubborn and not very understanding. When she gets upset, she gets very upset. She's just like that. Try and talk to her again, maybe at break."

This is so frustrating, thought Emily. I can't apologize to her if she just ignores me.

At that moment Samantha Lavigne marched up to the girls and stared at them, while she blew bubbles of bright-blue bubble gum. Her straight, blonde hair was tied tightly in a ponytail, and she was wearing too much make-up and enormous pink earrings.

ÜBUNG 6: Match-up. Was haben die Freundinnen gesagt und gedacht?

1. Evie says — that the situation is very frustrating.

2. Holly asks Emily — that Emily should talk to Evie.

3. Emily explains — that she has to see a teacher.

4. Nina asks Emily — that she's just so forgetful.

5. Emily says — to finish her sentence.

6. Nina says — if she had a nice weekend.

7. Emily thinks — that she has been thinking about *Seventh Heaven* a lot lately.

"Hi girls," she said. Her voice was full of fake friendliness. "How's it going?"

She didn't wait for the girls to answer; she just turned to Emily and said slyly, "I've just seen Michael Fernandez. He told me you got the part of Jenny. You must be surprised! Everybody thought I would get the part. I didn't even get the understudy part – they gave that part to Laura Padbury! I mean, oh my God – I didn't even know she could speak! Miss Moss has got it so wrong. But anyway, good luck."

She said the last two words very bitterly – it was clear that she did not really mean to wish Emily luck.

fake	unecht
slyly	listig
to require	erfordern, voraussetzen
to burst out laughing	in Gelächter ausbrechen
hilarious	wahnsinnig komisch

"Oh, thanks, Samantha," Emily replied. "So which part did you get?"

Samantha looked uncomfortable. "It's only a very small part. I'm... the lucky frog."

Emily, Holly and Nina smiled – it was hard not to laugh!

"Yes," continued Samantha, "I'm the frog. You probably want to laugh, but I know the part requires real talent – Miss Moss told me so. I only have four lines, but those four lines will be the best in the play."

She then turned away and marched back to her friends. Emily, Holly and Nina burst out laughing. "That's hilarious!" exclaimed Holly. "But Emily... is it true? Have you got the part of Jenny?"

Emily turned red. She had watched Nina's reaction to Samantha's news. Nina looked very disappointed. Nina wanted to be Jenny so much, thought Emily, so now I've upset another friend.

"Yes, I've got the part," Emily said quietly and with a small smile. "I'm sorry, Nina. I know you really wanted it."

Nina smiled, but only slightly. "It's okay," she said. "Well done, Emily. You'll make a great Jenny."

"Oh thanks, Nina. I'm so happy that I've got the part, you know. But I need to talk to Evie now."

"That's brilliant news, Emily!" cried Holly. She had an enormous smile on her face. It seemed like she was the only person who was genuinely happy.

The ringing of the school bell interrupted the girls; it was time for registration, so they picked up their bags and went into school.

ÜBUNG 7: Unscramble the words! Ordne die Buchstaben zu sinnvollen Wörtern.

1. isilahoru — h...........................
2. trainbill — b...........................
3. udrespris — s...........................
4. iplaynot — p...........................
5. tareconi — r...........................
6. morenosu — e...........................

At morning break Emily headed to her locker to get her chemistry book, ready for the next lesson. As she walked down the corridor towards the locker-room, she saw Michael walking towards her.

"Hey, Emily," he shouted, "or should I say 'Jenny'! I'm really excited about acting with you."

"Michael!" replied Emily. She was filled with a strange mixture of emotions: excitement but also nerves, just because he was talking to her. "Yeah, I can't wait to act with you either. It's going to be fun."

"Anyway, sorry, must dash," said Michael. "I'm playing football with the lads! See you soon!"

What an amazing boy! thought Emily. And was he flirting? Could he really like me, too? Maybe… just maybe…

But before she could begin to daydream about Michael, she saw Laura Padbury getting something from her locker.

"Hi Laura," said Emily, in a kind voice. "How are you doing?"

"Oh, hi… I'm fine thanks," answered Laura. "Well done for getting the part of Jenny! You must be so happy."

"Well, yes, I think I am happy, thanks," said Emily. "I mean, yes, I'm really happy, thanks."

genuinely	echt
to interrupt	unterbrechen
to head to(wards)	zusteuern auf
locker	Schließfach
emotion	Gefühl
excitement	Aufregung
nerves	Nervosität
I can't wait.	Ich freue mich darauf.
⚡ Must dash!	Ich muss los!
lad	Kumpel, Junge

"Good. I would be happy, too. I really wanted the part, but never mind."

"But you got the part of understudy, right? Well done for that! It's still an achievement. I'm really glad you're my understudy. I know you would do a great job if I couldn't do the play for some reason."

However, as Emily said these words, she knew they sounded false. She felt bad for Laura. She could tell Laura was disappointed. So many people were disappointed; so many people wanted the part! But for Laura it was different – she wanted to act. It was her hobby, the one thing she could do brilliantly. It wasn't just because of a crush.

achievement	Leistung
for some reason	aus irgendeinem Grund
false	unecht
to stick out	herausragen

"Anyway, bye, Emily," said Laura nervously, and walked off.

Emily knew that Laura wasn't going to meet any friends or go and play football. The fact was that Laura was going to spend break alone. Friends are so important, thought Emily as she walked over to her locker.

But Emily quickly forgot about Laura, because she noticed something very strange: A piece of paper was sticking out of the edge of her locker. What was it? Emily opened her locker, opened up the piece of paper and found a shocking message:

The message was written with letters from newspaper headlines, just like a ransom note.

I'm being threatened! thought Emily, alarmed. Who has written this? Who hates me so much?

Samantha? She's capable of something so horrible, and it's clear that she's bitter that I got the part.

Laura? She seems too innocent to make such a vicious threat... but the part is everything to her. And she is my understudy – she would definitely get the part if I stepped down. Besides, maybe that explains why

ransom note	Erpresserbrief
to threaten	bedrohen
alarmed	alarmiert, beunruhigt
capable of	fähig zu
bitter	verbittert
vicious	bösartig, gemein
threat	Drohung
to step down	zurücktreten

ÜBUNG 8: Which girl would be your best friend?
Finde heraus, mit welchem der Mädchen du dich am besten verstehen würdest!

1. You like spending your free time...
   a) ❑ looking in the mirror.
   b) ❑ hanging out with your closest friends.
   c) ❑ reading famous plays.
   d) ❑ being active – playing sport – meeting friends.

2. You walk past £20 in the street. You...
   a) ❑ spend it on make-up, hairspray and jewellery.
   b) ❑ don't see it – you're too busy daydreaming.
   c) ❑ leave it where it is – if people see you take it, they might think you are a thief!
   d) ❑ buy each of your friends a small present.

3. A young French girl joins your class, so you...
   a) ❑ laugh at her accent – it's so weird!
   b) ❑ tell her you think her accent is beautiful.
   c) ❑ daren't speak to her.
   d) ❑ begin a conversation *en français*!

she wanted to get away from me so quickly.

Or was it Evie? Is she so upset that I forgot her birthday that she would destroy my dreams? Emily felt so confused. Her head was spinning, full of names and motives. Who? And Why?

to spin	sich drehen
motive	Motiv, Beweggrund
⚡ to fancy sb.	auf jmd. stehen
actually	eigentlich, tatsächlich
⚡ What are you up to?	Was hast du vor?

"Emily!" cried a voice from behind her.

It was Nina. Emily put the note in her bag quickly, got her chemistry book out of her locker, then shut and locked it.

"How are you? I've just seen Michael – isn't he gorgeous? Every time I see him I think my crush gets bigger. I'm surprised *you* don't fancy him, too!"

Emily laughed to herself. Maybe I should actually tell Nina about my crush on Michael, she thought.

"Hi Nina, what are you up to?" Emily asked.

"I'm just on my way outside to meet Holly and Evie. They're in the usual place, by the steps to the sports hall. Come on, let's go together."

"I don't think that's a good idea. You see, I think Evie might hate me. I mean *really* hate me. You see…" Emily paused. Should she tell Nina about the threat? "You see… I've received a threat. And I think it could be from her."

"A threat?" replied Nina, almost laughing. "What do you mean, a threat? Evie wouldn't threaten you!"

ÜBUNG 9: Unscramble the sentences! Bringe die Satzteile in die richtige Reihenfolge, um die Drohungen zu entschlüsseln!

1. or I'll – your locker – keep quiet – blow up

....

2. tell everyone – town or – leave – your dirty secret – we'll

....

3. away from – steal – my boyfriend – stay – or I'll – yours

....

4. again – to you – never speak – give – or we'll – £20 – us

....

5. me – that text message – or – in the – show – throw – bag – your – river – I'll

....

....

....

Emily shook her head. "I think we should sit down, Nina. This might take a few minutes to explain."

canteen	Kantine
deaf	taub
joker	Spaßvogel

The girls walked into the school canteen, sat down at a table and put their bags on the other seats. Emily took the sheet of paper out of her bag. She passed it to Nina, and Nina read it aloud:

"'Step down from Jenny or else'? I don't understand. Where did you find this? And when?"

"Just now when I opened my locker... somebody must have pushed it inside."

"But Emily... this is not from Evie. It can't be. Evie wouldn't do this. It must be Samantha Lavigne. Yeah, Samantha Lavigne. She wants you to step down so that she can be Jenny. Or maybe it is even your understudy. What's her name? Oh yeah, Laura Padbury. But not Evie! Not our best friend Evie!"

Maybe Nina was right. Emily hoped that Nina was right.

"Listen, Emily," said Nina, "I'm just going to buy a drink, so wait here. I'll only be a minute."

Emily waited at the table while Nina went to buy a drink from the canteen counter. People in the canteen were chatting and laughing with their friends, just like normal.

Why can't today be just like normal for me? thought Emily. Why can't today be...

"Hey! Are you deaf?!" cried a voice. It was Owen Park, the school joker, who was standing with his gang of friends nearby. He thought that he was hilarious. His friends were all laughing, but Emily didn't find him very funny.

"Your phone is ringing! Aren't you going to answer it, you weirdo! Normal people answer their phone when it rings!"

"Okay, okay," replied Emily, "I can hear it. Now stop staring at me, you group of morons."

It wasn't actually Emily's phone that was ringing; it was Nina's.

Maybe it's Holly or Evie, thought Emily, so I should answer it.

ÜBUNG 10: Hidden words. Finde im Suchrätsel zehn Adjektive, die Personen beschreiben!

W	I	R	S	E	L	F	I	S	H	A	G	Y	C
U	R	N	Y	S	E	B	O	G	I	D	A	G	O
N	A	F	D	V	I	L	L	B	R	I	N	O	N
F	A	M	E	E	V	I	L	I	N	I	I	G	F
R	D	O	A	Q	P	C	K	N	Y	V	N	G	I
I	O	O	A	Z	U	E	R	O	I	O	G	D	D
E	U	E	M	I	I	F	N	V	E	Y	E	A	E
N	K	I	N	D	X	N	L	D	Q	C	O	R	N
D	S	I	H	U	A	S	G	L	E	A	A	I	T
L	S	T	U	B	B	O	R	N	Y	N	S	N	N
Y	P	S	J	N	O	E	S	Y	A	A	T	G	O

She opened up Nina's bag to look for her mobile phone. However, it was too late; the phone stopped ringing. Never mind, thought Emily, they'll ring back.

She began to close the bag, but as she did so she noticed something: a single sheet of newspaper. Once again, Emily was completely shocked. Nina?

Nina didn't read the newspaper, and she certainly never carried a single sheet of newspaper in her bag. There was only one possible explanation. Once again the words "Step down from Jenny or else" went through Emily's head. She began to get the sheet of newspaper out of Nina's bag. She wanted to look at it properly, so that she could see if letters were missing from the headlines. But then

⚡ weirdo	Spinner
⚡ moron	Trottel
completely shocked	total bestürzt
properly	richtig

she saw Nina coming back with her drink. Emily quickly put Nina's bag back.

"So, Emily," said Nina when she was back at the table, "do you believe me now? Evie didn't do this. How could one of your best friends do this?"

Exactly, thought Emily, how could one of my best friends do this?

"It must be Samantha," continued Nina, "because she's such a nasty person. Just ignore the note, Emily. I admit that I was upset that I didn't get the part of Jenny, but now I'm happy for you. You should definitely not step down from the part."

nasty	gemein
to admit	zugeben
two-faced	heuchlerisch
liar	Lügnerin
rehearsal	Probe
to deserve	verdienen
⚡ to play dirty	unfaire Mittel anwenden
victim	Opfer

You are such a two-faced liar, thought Emily.

"Now, come on," continued Nina, "let's go outside and find Holly and Evie."

But before they could go outside, the bell rang for the next lesson.

"Too late, morning break's over," said Emily. "I've got chemistry now, so I'll see you later. Bye!"

As Emily walked to her chemistry class, she made a decision. I will not step down from the part. I've not done anything to hurt Nina, and so I will not let her scare me. Tonight is the first rehearsal, and I will prove to everyone that I deserve this part. Of course, I need to show Evie that I am really sorry for forgetting her birthday, but I still deserve to play Jenny. And I want to act together with Michael... I deserve to act together with Michael.

> *ÜBUNG 11: Odd one out! Welches Wort ist das „schwarze Schaf"?*
>
> 1. now, today, yesterday, here
>
> 2. thought, wants, hoped, waited
>
> 3. go, chat, laugh, cry
>
> 4. bag, drink, paper, receive
>
> 5. moron, darling, weirdo, idiot
>
> 6. quickly, hilarious, good, normal
>
> 7. canteen, living room, sports hall, classroom

But it was also clear to Emily that the play had led to problems for the four friends.
I thought that *Seventh Heaven* was a chance for fun, she thought. But Nina has decided to play dirty. Well, I'm not going to be a victim of her dirty tricks.

For the first time that day, Emily was filled with confidence. She walked up the stairs, along the corridor and into the chemistry laboratory with a single thought in her head: A victim of Nina's dirty little tricks? Not me, no way.

> ÜBUNG 12: *True or false? Kreuze die richtigen Aussagen an!*
>
> 1. It wasn't Emily's phone that was ringing – it was Holly's. ❏
> 2. Emily only noticed the sheet of newspaper as she was closing Nina's bag. ❏
> 3. Nina tells Emily not to react to the note. ❏
> 4. Emily doesn't believe Nina when Nina says that she is happy for her. ❏
> 5. As soon as the girls were outside, the bell rang for the next lesson. ❏
> 6. Emily has a chemistry lesson next. ❏

There's Trouble in Seventh Heaven

3

Kurz vor der ersten Probe für das Theaterstück hat Emily immer noch nicht mit Evie geredet, die ihr weiter aus dem Weg geht. Aber gleich wird Emily endlich zusammen mit Michael auf der Bühne stehen – ihr Traum ist zum Greifen nahe! Das lässt sie fast den mysteriösen Drohbrief vergessen, zumal Andrew und Michael sich einig sind, dass nur Samantha den Brief geschrieben haben kann.
Während der Probe ist Emily nicht ganz bei der Sache, denn der Drohbrief geht ihr einfach nicht aus dem Kopf, und prompt hat Mr. Adams sie auf dem Kieker ...

That afternoon it was the first rehearsal of *Seventh Heaven* in the main school hall. The rehearsal was for everyone who was taking part – the cast, the costume designers, the stage crew, the

cast	Ensemble
costume designer	Kostümbildner
crew	Team
lighting	Beleuchtung
sound	Ton

lighting and sound team, and, of course, Mr Adams and Miss Moss, the directors. Everybody was talking to each other excitedly, discussing the different parts and reading

script	Skript (des Stücks)
set	Set, Bühnenbild
⚡ hiya	hey, hallo
distant	fern, weit weg
to suspect	den Verdacht haben, dass
to over-react	überreagieren
to refuse	ablehnen, sich weigern

the script. Emily arrived on her own but immediately saw Holly, who was one of the set designers.

"Hey, Holly!" cried Emily as she walked into the hall. "You alright?"

"Hiya, Emily. I'm fine, thanks," replied Holly. "I didn't see you at lunchtime. Evie, Nina and I were in the usual place – where were you?"

"I was with Andrew," Emily answered. "I wanted to talk to him about something. Something which I found in my locker this morning."

Emily usually spent every lunchtime with her three best friends. But on this particular day she felt distant from them. Of course, she suspected that Nina had written the threatening note, but she was also annoyed at Evie.

It was bad that I forgot Evie's birthday, she thought. But she has completely over-reacted. She ignores me when I see her. She refuses to answer my phone calls. She doesn't reply to my texts. I'll only apologize when she stops acting like a big baby.

At that moment, Evie and Nina walked into the hall. They were chatting to some of the other pupils taking part in the play. At the same time Mr Adams walked onto the stage and started to speak to everyone.

"Good afternoon everyone. Thank you for coming to the

first rehearsal of *Seventh Heaven*. Everyone must really concentrate during the rehearsals because the performances are only seven weeks away. Okay, let's get started. Costume designers, stage crew, lighting and sound team: go next door to Hall 2 with Miss Moss. All of the cast: stay here with me. Everyone in scene one, on stage now, please!"

"What? What did you find in your locker?" Holly asked Emily. "Quick! I've got to go into Hall 2!"

"I'll tell you later, Holly," Emily said quickly. "But listen: I don't want people to find out about this thing which I found in my locker. So don't tell anyone. Promise?"

to concentrate	sich konzentrieren
let's get started	lasst uns loslegen
straight away	sofort, unverzüglich
to mention	erwähnen
to keep one's promises	seine Versprechen halten
villain	Bösewicht
suited	passend, geeignet

Holly looked very confused. "Okay, promise," she replied. Holly didn't have time for any more questions. She had to follow the other set designers into Hall 2. Evie was going into this hall, too; she was one of the costume designers. Naturally, she began to chat to Holly straight away as they walked into Hall 2. However, Emily knew that Holly would not mention the note. Holly always kept her promises.

Although she had not got the part of Jenny, Nina still wanted to take part in the play, so she had accepted another part in the play; "Emma-Jayne Maynard", the play's villain, who constantly tries to split up Reece and Jenny.

This part would be more suited to Samantha Lavigne, Nina thought to herself, quietly laughing. Samantha wouldn't have to act – she's just like the character in real life!

Nina smiled at Emily and shouted to her across the hall. "Hey Emily, I've got something to show you."

ÜBUNG 13: Prepositions. Vervollständige die Sätze mit den passenden Präpositionen!

| in | into | to | onto | amongst | with | for |

1. The first play rehearsal was .... everyone involved.

2. Emily had found something .... her locker.

3. Emily usually spent every lunchtime .... Holly, Evie and Nina.

4. Nina and Evie walked .... the hall.

5. Mr Adams walked .... the stage.

6. He thanked everyone for coming .... the rehearsal.

7. .... the people going into Hall 2 was Evie.

plain	gewöhnlich
affection	Zuneigung
deliberately	mit Absicht
⚡ mate	Kumpel

"Not now, Nina!" demanded Mr Adams. "You're Emma-Jayne Maynard, aren't you? So quickly, get on stage now!"

"We're not in scene one, are we, Emily?" said a sexy, smooth voice from behind Emily. It could only be one person…

"Hi Michael!" replied Emily. Emily loved it when he called her by her name. *Emily*. Such a plain name… but when Michael Fernandez said it, it was more than a name. It was a personal touch, almost a sign of affection.

"No," Emily continued, "we're not in the play until scene two, Michael." She used his name deliberately, just as she loved it when Michael used her name, she loved using his name, too.

"Then let's go and sit down," said Michael. "Maybe over there with Andrew Howard."

They went and sat down next to Andrew, who was sitting on his own at the back of the hall.

"Hey Andy!" said Michael. "How's it going, mate?"

"Errrm, I'm fine, thanks, Michael, how are you?" replied Andrew.

Andy? thought Andrew. Nobody ever calls me *Andy*! Usually I'm just plain Andrew. And nobody ever calls me *mate*!

"Not bad, not bad at all, mate," replied Michael.

The three teenagers began to talk about the play. Emily was happy to talk to people who were not mad at her. On the stage the actors in scene one were reading through the script for the first time. Emily, Michael and Andrew quietly made comments about the actors. Who would be a good actor? Some people were terribly characterless! This made all three of them laugh.

As the scene went on, Andrew became less impressed by Michael and more jealous of him. Emily's a different person when he's around, he thought. But Andrew was very rational and not easily

to be mad at sb.	auf jmd. wütend sein
impressed	beeindruckt
rational	vernünftig

bothered by such things. I suppose it is just typical girly behaviour, he sighed to himself.

Emily was, indeed, feeling closer and closer to Michael. She knew that she could trust Andrew; he already knew about the threatening note from their conversation at lunchtime. And now she believed she could tell Michael.

If I tell him about the note, she thought, that'll show him I trust him. This way we'll get even closer.

"Michael, remember when I saw you at break?" Emily asked.

"Yes," he replied, "I certainly do."

"Well, when I went to my locker after that, I found this inside it," said Emily, and got the piece of paper out of her bag:

"What on earth...?" said Michael, clearly shocked. "Is this a joke?"

"If it is a joke," replied Emily, "then it's not a very funny one."

"But... I don't understand." Michael paused to think for a few moments, then he continued, "Who would do such a thing? Who would threaten you, just for a part in a school play?"

"I think I know who," said Emily, "and it's really upset me. I think it might be Nina. I saw a piece of newspaper in her

bag... newspaper... the note... it all adds up. But she's one of my best friends. So, I'm really confused... I just don't get it."
"Nina? But why would she?" asked Michael.
Before Emily had chance to answer the question, Andrew interrupted, "I don't think it's Nina. There is a rational explanation for the newspaper in her bag, surely. I think it's Samantha Lavigne. She's nasty enough to do something like this. Nina isn't. She just isn't."

indeed	tatsächlich
to trust sb.	jmd. vertrauen
what on earth	was zum Teufel
to add up	einen Sinn ergeben
⚡ to get it	etw. verstehen
proof	Beweis

"I think I agree with Andrew," said Michael. "Newspaper in her bag? That isn't proof, Emily."
"I don't know," said Emily. "I really don't. I don't know for sure if it is Nina, or Samantha, or anyone else who has threatened me. I only know one thing: I am not going to step down from this part."
Michael smiled at Emily, a smile which said: "That's right! Don't step down!"
But the teenagers didn't have time to discuss the threat any more, because it was time for scene two.

"Okay! Next scene!" said Mr Adams. "I want Reece and Jenny on stage... so that's Michael Fernandez and Emily Etchells, on stage now, quickly! Andrew Howard and Laura Padbury, come down to the front. Since you two are the understudies, you need to get into the roles of Reece and

ÜBUNG 14: Reading comprehension. Beantworte die folgenden Fragen zur Geschichte!

1. What did Emily do at lunchtime?

....

2. Which character is Nina playing in *Seventh Heaven*?

....

3. Which adjectives are used to describe Michael Fernandez's voice?

....

4. Why does Andrew become jealous of Michael as the scene goes on?

....

5. Why does Emily believe that Nina is threatening her?

....

6. Does Andrew think that Nina is threatening Emily?

....

Jenny from the beginning, too."

Emily was excited. The beginning of Reece and Jenny! The beginning of Michael and Emily? Maybe!

briefcase	Aktentasche
Mr Popular	jmd., der sehr beliebt ist
audience	Publikum
to consider sth.	etw. beachten, an etw. denken

"Oh, first of all, I have something for you two," shouted Mr Adams to Emily and Michael.

Mr Adams walked off the stage, picked up his briefcase and walked to the back of the hall, where they were sitting.

"This is a sheet with tips for learning your lines, since you both have so many. Read it tonight at home."

Michael and Emily put the sheets of paper in their bags and followed Mr Adams, who had left his briefcase wide open on the seat next to Emily's bag.

"This is the scene where Jenny first meets Reece in the park," explained Mr Adams. "Remember, Jenny is new in town, so she's quiet and shy. Reece, however, is Mr Popular. The audience must understand this, so consider this every time you say a line. You can really show your character's feelings and personality through your tone of voice."

As Mr Adams described the setting and the characters, Emily noticed Evie, who was coming into the hall through the back door.

Oh, thought Emily, the meeting in the other hall with Miss Moss must have finished.

Emily continued to watch Evie. She was standing by Emily's bag and was chatting to Alexa Fletcher, one of the other costume designers.

envelope	Briefumschlag
curiously	neugierig
desperately	unbedingt
to hesitate	zögern
there was real chemistry	die Chemie stimmte
to glare at	anstarren
bully	Tyrann

I hope she stays until the end of the rehearsal, thought Emily, then I can definitely see her and apologize.

Then Evie put something in Emily's bag. It was difficult to see this object, but it looked like an envelope.

What could it be? thought Emily, curiously. She desperately wanted to go and see what it was. But not now! she thought. What would Mr Adams think?

"Emily, are you listening?" asked Mr Adams.

"Of course, sir," answered Emily, although she clearly wasn't.

"Then what did I just say?"

"Errrm…"

"Exactly. You weren't listening. If you don't concentrate, I will not hesitate to give your part to someone else. I need one hundred percent concentration from you. Do you understand?"

"Yes, sir," answered Emily.

Mr Adams finished his explanation, and Michael and Emily began scene two.

I've got to forget about Evie for the moment, thought Emily, and concentrate on being Jenny.

This was quite easy, because Emily was so happy to begin acting with Michael. On the outside, Emily became Jenny –

quiet, shy and unsure. But on the inside she was smiling wildly. Reece and Jenny! Michael and Emily!

Very soon Michael and Emily were reading the last few lines of the scene:

> *Jenny:* It's getting late. I've got to go home now, or my dad will be mad.
> *Reece:* Okay, but please, come to my party on Friday night. The whole school's gonna be there.
> *Jenny:* I don't know. My dad doesn't let me go to parties at night. And definitely not boys' parties.
> *Reece:* Come on, Jenny – Go wild! Play dangerously! Come to my party. It's gonna be the party of the century... especially for you. I promise.
> *Jenny:* Okay, I'll try to come. I'll try. I promise.
> *Reece:* No 'maybes', baby. You'll be there.
> *Jenny:* Goodbye, Reece. I'll... see you around.
> *Reece:* You certainly will, baby. You certainly will.

"Right," said Mr Adams. "That was good. There was real chemistry between Reece and Jenny."

That's because there's chemistry between me and Michael, thought Emily.

"With your full concentration it would be even better," continued Mr Adams, as he glared at Emily.

"Now, let's quickly read through scene three. Michael, you may sit down – you're not in this scene. But Emily, stay on stage. And I need Emma-Jayne, plus the two bullies, Helen and Marie, on stage, too. Quickly!"

Nina and the two girls who were playing Helen and Marie got up and came onto the stage. After the day's events, Emily was worried about acting alongside Nina. She was suspicious of her, even if Michael and Andrew weren't.

"Okay, let's start," said Mr Adams when all of the actors were on stage.

"What did you want to show me before?" Emily whispered to Nina. Perhaps it could explain the day's strange events?

"Emily!" shouted Mr Adams. "You're not concentrating, *again*! This is your last warning. I will not tell you to concentrate again – next time I'll just ask you to leave and not come back."

"I'm sorry, sir," answered Emily. "I promise I'll concentrate now."

alongside	Seite an Seite mit, neben
suspicious	misstrauisch, argwöhnisch
to whisper	flüstern
obvious	offensichtlich

The scene went quite smoothly. Emily felt awkward when she was acting with Nina, but luckily it wasn't obvious. At 4.30, the rehearsal came to an end.

"Thank you for today, everyone," said Mr Adams. "Begin learning your lines straight away. Everyone needs to be able to act without their script as soon as possible."

ÜBUNG 15: Can you trust your crush? Finde heraus, ob du deinem Schwarm deine Geheimnisse anvertrauen kannst!

1. The boy you have a crush on spends morning break...
   a) ❏ laughing with his friends.
   b) ❏ playing football.
   c) ❏ volunteering as an anti-bullying counsellor.

2. He likes talking to girls who are...
   a) ❏ pretty.
   b) ❏ friendly, interesting and fun.
   c) ❏ sensitive, kind and believers in true friendship.

3. Your friend falls over at school and everyone nearby starts to laugh loudly. The boy...
   a) ❏ is laughing the loudest.
   b) ❏ just walks past and does nothing.
   c) ❏ tells everyone to stop laughing.

He then turned to Miss Moss, who was sat at the front of the hall. "How did your meeting go, Melissa?"

caretaker	Hausmeister
odd	merkwürdig, seltsam
meanwhile	mittlerweile
to make one's way	gehen, sich begeben

"It went well. We've got a good technical team this year. I just need to ask the caretaker if we can use Hall 2 on Friday. Have you got his phone number?"

"Yeah, I think so. Let me just check... errrm, where did I leave my phone? Oh, in my briefcase."

Mr Adams walked to the back of the hall to find his briefcase open, but without a mobile phone inside.

"That's odd," he said. "Where's my phone?"

"I'll ring it," said Miss Moss, "and then you'll hear where it is."

Miss Moss took out her mobile phone and began to ring Mr Adams' phone number.

Meanwhile, most of the actors were picking up their bags and slowly making their way out of the hall, although Emily, Nina and the girls playing Helen and Marie were still on stage, chatting about the scene.

"Whose bag is this?" Miss Moss demanded, as she picked up Emily's bag and held it in the air. The phone was ringing from the bag, as clearly as a bell.

"It's... mine, Miss," said Emily, slowly. "But I've got no idea whose phone is inside."

ÜBUNG 16: Verb forms. Ergänze die Sätze mit der korrekten Verbform!

1. The two girls who *(play)* .... Helen and Marie came onto the stage.

2. Mr Adams opened up his briefcase and *(take)* .... out two sheets of paper.

3. Emily *(notice)* .... Evie, who was coming into the hall through the back door.

4. This is the scene where Jenny first *(meet)* .... Reece in the park.

5. Emily *(feel)* .... awkward when she was acting with Nina.

6. I *(need)* .... to ask the caretaker something.

"It's *my* phone!" shouted Mr Adams. "That is my ring-tone! Emily Etchells, explain yourself immediately! What on earth is my mobile phone doing in your bag?"

ring-tone	Klingelton
to quit	aufhören mit, aufgeben

"I... I... I don't know! I didn't put it there!" Then she remembered. Evie!

"It wasn't me, sir, I promise. But I think I know who did it. Somebody is threatening me – someone wants me to quit the play. Look, I can prove it. Look inside my bag – there's a note I found in my locker today, a note threatening me."

Evie, Emily thought, Evie put something into my bag. But why would she put Mr Adams' mobile into my bag? She's my best friend! Miss Moss opened Emily's bag fully and looked inside.

thief	Dieb
sensitively	einfühlsam
to set sb. up	hereinlegen
to nod	nicken
unless	wenn nicht, falls nicht
to beg	betteln
to stick by sb.	zu jmd. halten

"Emily," she said, "there's no note in here. There are just your schoolbooks, pencil case… and Mr Adams' phone. I want to believe you Emily, but…"

"She's clearly a thief!" said Mr Adams, much less sensitively.

"I'm *not* a thief! I've been set up," replied Emily. "Honestly, I promise. There *was* a note in my bag. My friends have seen it – Nina, Andrew, Michael… tell Mr Adams – there *was* a note!"

Nina, Andrew and Michael all nodded.

"Emily's not a liar, sir," said Nina, "and she's not a thief. We all saw the note. It told Emily to 'step down from Jenny, or else'."

"Well," said Mr Adams, "I'm afraid I don't believe you. Because now, it seems to me that you *are* a thief, Emily. And until you can prove you are not, I don't want you in my play. Besides, your concentration today was awful. I need better."

He then turned to Laura Padbury. "Laura, unless Emily Etchells can prove that she's not a thief, you'll play Jenny."

"No, sir!" cried Emily. "No, sir! Please, sir! You *have* to believe me! Please, sir! *Please, sir*!"

But begging was useless. Mr Adams refused to change his mind.

"Don't worry," said Nina. "We'll stick by you. We'll prove to everyone that you're not a thief and that you're the right Jenny. Somehow."

Emily began to cry. "How could it all go so wrong, Nina?" she asked her friend. "How?" The two girls walked out of the hall and into the schoolyard, and Michael and Andrew followed in silence. Emily felt physically sick with fear, anger and sadness. As she walked, she felt her dream, which had been so close, slip further and further away.

to slip away	weggleiten, schwinden

ÜBUNG 17: Unscramble the text! Ordne die folgenden Sätze chronologisch!

a) Nina tells Mr Adams that she saw the note.

b) Emily begs Mr Adams to believe her.

c) Emily tells the teachers to look inside her bag.

d) Emily begins to cry.

e) Mr Adams asks Laura to play Jenny.

f) Miss Moss opens Emily's bag, but there is no note inside it.

1	2	3	4	5	6
c					

Secrets and Milkshakes

4

Emily ist verzweifelt, dass sie nicht die Jenny spielen darf, aber noch mehr macht ihr zu schaffen, dass ausgerechnet Evie ihr heimlich Mr. Adams Handy in ihre Tasche gesteckt hat. Nicht nur ihr Theatertraum, auch ihre Freundschaften scheinen sich in Luft aufzulösen!
Auf dem Weg zur Schule erzählt Emily Andrew von ihrem Verdacht. Als Andrew ihr rät, mit Evie über alles zu reden, steht diese plötzlich hinter ihnen. Sie hat alles gehört …

"We're lucky again," said the Radio DJ. "It's going to be another beautiful day. We've got more of today's hottest dance and R & B on the way, but first, here's Newsreader Kev with the headlines…"
"No!" cried Emily, and hit her radio alarm clock to turn it off. "Nooooooooo! Go away, Tuesday! I'm staying in bed. I'm not getting up today!"
Yesterday morning was bad, she thought, but this morning is a thousand times worse. The whole school thinks I'm a thief, I don't have a part in *Seventh Heaven*, and worst of all, these problems are all because of my best friend Evie. I've lost my best friend.

Slowly and reluctantly, Emily got up, got ready for school, walked round to Andrew's house and knocked on his door. Once again, Andrew opened the door straight away and was ready to go to school.

newsreader	Nachrichtensprecher
headlines	Schlagzeilen
reluctantly	widerstrebend
suspicion	Verdacht, Verdächtigung
in private	unter vier Augen
devastated	am Boden zerstört

"Ready?" he asked Emily.

"Ready," replied Emily, without any enthusiasm at all, and they set off to school. It was clear that Emily did not want to talk, so Andrew did not even bother to ask any questions. But when they arrived at school, Emily decided she had to tell somebody about her suspicions.

"Andrew, you know that I'm upset because I've lost my part in the play. But there's another reason why I'm upset. Let's go behind the sports hall so that I can tell you in private."

They walked behind the sports hall and sat at the bottom of the steps which led to the tennis courts.

"It's Evie. I think she put Mr Adams' phone in my bag. I saw her. But... I thought I could trust her," Emily said. "Evie's one of my closest friends. I'm upset about losing the part, and I'm really upset that people think I am a thief. But I am devastated that my friendship means absolutely nothing to Evie. I can't believe Evie would do something so nasty, so awful. If I can't trust Evie, who can I trust? Nobody at all," Emily sighed.

"Are you *sure* Evie did it?" Andrew asked.
"I think so. I saw her put something in my bag!"
"Then you need to talk to her and ask her why she did it. It will help, Emily, honestly. You need to..."
Suddenly, a voice behind them interrupted Andrew, "But you *don't* know it was me," it said. It was Evie. She was standing on the steps with Nina and Holly, staring at Emily.
"How could you think that I would... that I would ever hurt you?" Evie continued. "Emily, you're my oldest friend. I'm so sorry I was mad at you for forgetting my birthday. I'm really, really sorry. I was mad, Emily, but I would never

threaten you or make you look like a thief. Why do you think that I would? I don't understand."
Emily turned red with embarrassment. Evie heard every word I just said! she thought.
"Oh, Evie... I saw you, Evie," answered Emily, as she walked up the steps to the girls. "I saw you: you were chatting to Alexa Fletcher and then you put something into my bag. Don't deny it."
"Emily, you've got it wrong," said Nina. "We're talking about Evie. Evie would *never* do that!"
"Yeah, you didn't put anything into Emily's bag, did you, Evie?" Holly added.
Evie paused for a second and then replied, "In fact, I did put something into your bag, Emily. But it wasn't Mr Adams' mobile. It was a letter."

Then Emily remembered. It looked like a piece of paper, or maybe an envelope, she thought. Maybe Evie is telling the truth. Emily didn't know what to say. "It was a letter to apologize," said Evie, "for being so pathetic and refusing to speak to you. If you don't believe me, ask Alexa. Wasn't it in your bag?"

embarrassment	Verlegenheit
to deny	bestreiten
pathetic	erbärmlich
to accuse	anklagen

"No," replied Emily, quietly. She was quickly realizing how wrong she was. "Whoever put the phone in my bag must have taken the letter out. And they took out the threat, too. Oh Evie... I'm so sorry. Firstly I forgot your birthday, and secondly I accused you of threatening me and making me look like a thief. I've been so upset since yesterday – I thought you hated me. I was so scared that I had lost your friendship forever. I'm so sorry. How could I think such things?"

"It's okay," said Evie. "Honestly. Friends?"

"Friends!" answered Emily, and the two girls hugged. Holly and Nina smiled with relief.

ÜBUNG 18: Fill in the right word! Ergänze die Sätze mit dem passenden Wort.

with   anyone   everything   any   everyone

1. Emily believed that .... in the school thought she was a thief.

2. Emily didn't want to talk, so Andrew decided not to ask her .... questions.

3. Emily told Andrew that if she couldn't trust Evie, then she couldn't trust ....

4. Evie had heard .... Emily had just said.

5. When Evie and Emily hugged, Holly and Nina smiled .... relief.

"Anyway, I need to thank you," said Evie. "Thank you for the message in the newspaper from you, Holly and Nina. It was a lovely thing to do."

to hug	(sich) umarmen
announcements page	Anzeigenseite
I told you so.	Ich hab's dir doch gesagt.
to solve	lösen (Problem)

"Oh yeah," said Nina, and reached into her bag. "That's what I wanted to show you yesterday, Emily. Remember? During the rehearsal?"

Nina pulled a sheet of newspaper out of her bag. A notice in the announcements page was circled:

> **HAPPY BIRTHDAY EVIE!**
>
> *Have a fantastic day!*
> Love from your best friends in
> the *WHOLE WORLD*!!
> Holly, Emily and Nina x x x

Oh no! thought Emily. How wrong could I be! That's the newspaper page I saw in Nina's bag yesterday. Oh, I'm so stupid!

She turned to Andrew, who smiled at her – a smile which said 'I told you so'.

"Oh, it's okay, Evie, you're welcome." Emily then turned to Nina, and her face became red with embarrassment. "Thanks for showing me, Nina. It looks great, doesn't it?"

"Yeah," Nina replied. "But anyway, now we have another problem to solve. Who *is* responsible for threatening Emily? How can we find out?"

"Everyone needs to keep their eyes open and look for any suspicious behaviour," Holly said.

"And you should continue going to the rehearsals," said Andrew, pointing at Emily. "Even if you just watch the rehearsal. That way, you will learn the part of Jenny more quickly when you are proven innocent."

"Okay, I will do," said Emily. Plus, she thought, smiling to herself, rehearsal-time is Michael-time!

to sew	nähen
to distract	ablenken
nevertheless	trotzdem, nichtsdestoweniger
to memorize	auswendig lernen
gesture	Geste

The days and the weeks passed by, and the date of the first performance of the play came closer and closer. Nina, Evie and Holly worked on the play; learning lines, sewing costumes and painting the set. But they also spent a lot of time outside rehearsals with Emily – they wanted to distract her from the play, so that she didn't feel left out. They went ice-skating, saw a couple of films at the cinema and even went to a concert.

"You know, Emily," said Holly, as they were leaving the concert, "who needs a stupid school play when we can do such brilliant things together."

Nevertheless, Emily followed Andrew's advice and continued to go to every rehearsal. She watched Laura play the part of Jenny, and she memorized the movements, actions and gestures. Whenever Mr Adams and Miss Moss gave Laura tips, Emily wrote the tips down in her notepad. But as she watched Michael and Laura on stage together, Emily felt very jealous. Emily hated feeling jealous – she simply wasn't a jealous type of person. But in this situation – when Michael was looking into Laura's eyes – jealousy was Emily's only possible reaction.

Samantha Lavigne became Laura's understudy (as well as continuing to play the frog). So she, too, learnt the part of Jenny, just like Andrew learnt the part of Reece. In their spare time, Emily and Andrew practised "Jenny's" scenes, so that Emily had as much practice at being Jenny as possible.

Before long, the first performance was only a week away. The girls still had no evidence to indicate who was responsible for the threat in Emily's locker and putting Mr Adams' phone in her bag. They did, however, have their suspicions. "It *must* be Samantha Lavigne," Evie said to Emily, Michael and Andrew, when they were watching a rehearsal of scene three. "Just look at her. She's so nasty to Laura – I think Samantha will start sending threats to *her*! And besides – who wants to be a frog?!"

"Actually, I'm not so sure that it was Samantha," replied Michael. "Maybe it was Laura. She's the one who has gained the most – she's got the part of Jenny! Maybe her quietness is an act – acting is her talent, after all."

evidence	Beweis
to indicate	(an)zeigen
to gain	erlangen, gewinnen
act	Theater, Show

ÜBUNG 19: Crossword. Löse das Kreuzworträtsel!

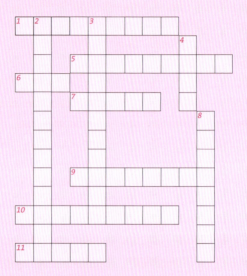

1. You can buy it every day to read articles about new events.
2. The emotion when you feel uncomfortable and your face turns red.
3. The premiere of a play is its first ... in front of an audience.
4. A piece of paper which is part of a book or newspaper.
5. Fantastic, great, extremely good.
6. You carry it with you to keep things in.
7. Another word for Planet Earth: The ...
8. The day in each year when you become one year older.
9. Not guilty.
10. The day before today.
11. In a theatre, the audience watches the actors on ...

He's so wise, thought Emily. Michael is friendly, handsome and so romantic, but he's also very clever! It's true that Laura has gained the most. Nevertheless, Emily still suspected Samantha the most.

"I'm sure she had the chance to get away from the stage at some point," said Michael. "And then she could have put the phone in your bag. Maybe she went to the toilet. Maybe she went to her bag, very briefly. You don't know for certain that she was always at the front of the hall, for the whole rehearsal."

wise	klug
monologue	Monolog
to fold one's arms	die Arme verschränken
prime suspect	Hauptverdächtige

"Maybe you're right, but I still think it was probably Samantha," replied Emily. "Just look at her!"

They all turned to look at the stage. Laura was acting out a very emotional and perfectly acted monologue. Samantha was standing with her arms folded, glaring at her. It was clear that Samantha was jealous... she didn't try to hide it!

For Emily, Evie and Andrew, Samantha was the prime suspect. But Michael continued to argue that Laura was capable of threatening Emily and making her look like a thief.

"I am just saying that Laura Padbury is quiet, not an angel," said Michael, at the end of the rehearsal. "And you know what people say: 'The quiet ones are always the worst.'"

At that moment Laura tapped Michael on the shoulder. "I'll... errrm... see you tomorrow, Michael," she said nervously. "I've... errrm... I've really enjoyed acting with you today." She blushed.

Emily felt full of jealousy. Flirting with 'her' Michael! Michael's right, the quiet ones are always the worst, Emily thought.

to tap	tippen, klopfen
to blush	erröten
fabric	Stoff
That's good of you.	Das ist nett von dir.

As the friends said goodbye to one another, Evie realized she had forgotten Samantha's frog costume.

"I need to sew some buttons onto it at home. I'll go back for it now," she told her friends. "So, see you all tomorrow."

"Bye!" everyone replied and set off home.

When Evie reached the hall, Samantha was just leaving. She began to wave some green fabric in the air.

"You forgot this!" she cried to Evie. It was her frog costume.

"Oh, thanks Samantha," replied Evie, slightly surprised at this nice gesture. "That's good of you."

"Well, I need it to be finished, don't I!" Samantha replied with a smile. A false smile or a genuine smile? Evie was unsure.

"You know, I was quite surprised to see you talking to Emily Etchells today," continued Samantha. "I heard that she accused you of stealing Mr Adams' mobile phone a few weeks ago... and you are still friends? Don't you hate her for saying such a nasty thing about you?"

ÜBUNG 20: Choose the right verb! Unterstreiche jeweils das passende der drei Verben.

1. Samantha continues to do/make/play the frog.

2. The first performance became/was/stood only a week away.

3. Although they had no evidence, the girls had/made/thought their suspicions.

4. Michael claimed that Laura had claimed/gained/received the most from Emily being kicked out of the play.

5. Michael said Laura could have put/stood/sat the phone in Emily's bag.

6. "Maybe you have/make/are right," said Emily.

7. I'm just saying/telling/talking that Laura is quiet, not an angel.

Evie almost told Samantha that she and Emily were still good friends, but then she had an idea. Maybe, she thought, if I pretend that I hate Emily, Samantha will think I am on her side and

to pretend	so tun, als ob
to confess	gestehen
⚡ to kick out	rausschmeißen
to congratulate	gratulieren
to work	*hier:* funktionieren
⚡ to hang out	abhängen
to get oneself into hot water	in Teufels Küche kommen

then she might confess everything to me. Maybe...
"Oh yes, I do hate her," Evie lied to Samantha. "I just pretend to be her friend so that I can spend time with Holly and Nina. But really, I think she's pathetic. She's paranoid and crazy. When she accused me of putting Mr Adams' phone in her bag, I realized that she doesn't deserve to be in the play. So I am glad that she got kicked out. And do you know what...?"
"What?" asked Samantha, curiously.
"I don't know who threatened Emily and put the phone in her bag. But if I did know, I would congratulate that person."
Evie felt awful for telling such enormous lies. But this might work, she thought. This might get Emily back in the play!
"Wow!" said Samantha, shocked. "I had no idea you were so mad at her! Hey, after the rehearsal on Saturday, do you fancy hanging out, maybe going for a milkshake?"
"Errrm... yeah, definitely sounds great!" Oh no! Evie thought. Am I getting myself into hot water?

"Great! Well, see you later."
"Okay, see you later, Samantha!"
"Bye... oh, Evie... please, call me Sammy."

The next day, Evie told Emily, Holly and Nina about what she had said to Samantha. She was worried that her friends might be angry, but all three of them took the news well.

"I think it's a great plan and I have another idea," said Emily. "Take my dictaphone with you on Saturday so you can record her... if she confesses, then we can use it as proof. I really don't think that I have much chance of acting in the play now – the play is next week, and so it is too late to make big changes. But I still want to prove my innocence."

"You're right," added Holly. "We four friends will show the school who the real culprit is."

Saturday was the final day of preparation for *Seventh Heaven* before the first performance on Monday. Holly and the set designers finished painting the scenery, and Evie and the costume designers finished sewing the trousers and skirts, blouses and shirts. Nina and the cast had a full dress rehearsal, and Emily followed all of Laura's lines and actions perfectly.

After the rehearsal began *Evie's* acting. She chatted with Samantha and ignored her friends.

dictaphone	Diktiergerät
to record	aufzeichnen
culprit	Täter, Schuldige
scenery	Kulisse

ÜBUNG 21: Multiple choice. Wähle die richtige Fortsetzung zu jedem Satzanfang!

1. Evie realizes she has forgotten...
   a) ❏ some buttons.
   b) ❏ Samantha's frog costume.
   c) ❏ to say goodbye to her friends.

2. Evie pretends that she hates Emily, because she thinks Samantha might...
   a) ❏ decide she hates Emily, too.
   b) ❏ spend time with Holly and Nina.
   c) ❏ tell Evie that she is responsible for putting Mr Adams' phone in Emily's bag.

3. Evie feels awful because...
   a) ❏ she's simply talking to Samantha Lavigne.
   b) ❏ she really does think Emily is crazy.
   c) ❏ she is telling such huge lies.

4. Oh no! thought Evie, Am I getting myself into...
   a) ❏ hot water?
   b) ❏ a new friendship?
   c) ❏ the bath?

secretly	heimlich
⚡ chitchat	Geplauder
to keep a secret	ein Geheimnis bewahren
to cheer	jauchzen, jubeln
⚡ to bop around	herumspringen
dare	*hier:* Wette

"Let's go to Sankey's café for that milkshake," she said. "I went there for my birthday — you can get these really amazing milkshake cocktails. It's cool."

"Yeah, sounds great," answered Samantha, and the two girls headed to the café. They ordered their milkshakes and sat down, and Evie secretly pressed the play button on the dictaphone. *Click*. It would record every word Samantha said. At first this was just general chitchat about school, friends and boys. But soon, after only five minutes, Samantha said something which suddenly made Evie extremely interested.

"I have something to tell you, Evie," said Samantha, and then whispered, "Something which you must keep a secret. You mustn't tell anyone."

"Okay, Sammy, I can keep a secret."

Samantha began to whisper to Evie, but within seconds she was interrupted: The boys at the table behind them started cheering, laughing and shouting. Samantha and Evie turned round. Owen Park was bopping around like a fool, dancing to the music in the café.

One of the boys turned to Samantha and explained that it was a dare: They would buy him a milkshake if he got up and did a stupid dance. At first, Samantha laughed at Owen's dancing, but then he

carelessly bumped into Evie and Samantha's table and knocked Samantha's milkshake all over her.
"You idiot!" cried Samantha. "You complete idiot! Look at me! I'm covered in milkshake."
"Don't get stressed," Owen replied. "I'll buy you another. Was it the mint one – a 'Green Monster'?"
"I don't want another, you fool. Evie, I'm going home to get changed. See you on Monday."
"But Sammy... what did you want to tell me?" shouted Evie, as Samantha hurried out of the café.
Samantha didn't reply. I don't even know her number, so I can't ask her on the phone, Evie thought. I'll have to wait until Monday for Samantha to finally confess.

Monday arrived. The waiting was over. After weeks of hard work, it was time for the first performance of *Seventh Heaven*.

When Evie arrived at school that morning, she found her friends as quickly as possible and giddily told

carelessly	sorglos
to bump into sth.	mit etw. zusammenstoßen
covered in	verschmiert mit
to hurry	eilen
giddily	benommen vor Aufregung
anxiety	Angst, Unruhe

them about everything which had happened in the café. "She told me that I couldn't tell anyone – that it was a secret! She must want to tell me that she put the phone in your bag, Emily, she *must*!" Evie said, with a mixture of excitement and anxiety.

ÜBUNG 22: Unscramble the words! Ordne die Buchstaben zu sinnvollen Wörtern!

1. kluciqy   q............................
2. tienxay   a............................
3. tecarhacr   c............................
4. ancediue   a............................
5. icdecant   a............................
6. fonsces   c............................

Evie spent the whole day trying to find Samantha. She has to confess before the play tonight! she thought. But she couldn't find her anywhere during the day, and had to wait until the evening of the performance.

| to dye | färben |
| hood | Kapuze |

The actors arrived early in the evening to prepare. Nina was reading through her lines for a final time. Holly and Evie were helping with the make-up, and Michael and Laura were discussing their scenes together. Andrew was standing at the hall entrance, ready to check people's tickets, because his character, Mr Neville, wasn't in the play until the second act.

Emily, of course, wasn't preparing for the play. She was in the audience – the first person to arrive. I tried very hard to get my part in the play back, she thought. But it didn't work, so I have to accept that.

When Samantha arrived, she had dyed her hair green – perfect for her role as the frog.

"Sammy!" cried Evie, as she walked through the door. "I love your hair... it's so 'froggish'! Here's your costume. And by the way, what did you want to tell me on Saturday... before the milkshake accident?"

"Not now, Evie!" Samantha replied. "I've got to get my costume and make-up on! I'll tell you once I'm ready, okay?"

Ten minutes later, Samantha was ready. She asked Evie to go outside with her. She put her black coat on, and put her hood up so that the audience would not see her green face, hair and costume, and the two girls walked outside.

ÜBUNG 23: Mr Right. Welcher Junge wäre dein Traumfreund – Michael Fernandez, Andrew Howard oder Owen Park?

1. Where would your dream boy take you on your first date?
   a) ❏ An ice-cream parlour – you can chat and get to know each other in a nice atmosphere.
   b) ❏ A football match.
   c) ❏ An expensive restaurant – the boy would pay of course.

2. What present would your dream boyfriend give you for your birthday?
   a) ❏ A homemade card – he has put a lot of time, effort and thought into it.
   b) ❏ A DVD of a funny film.
   c) ❏ Diamond earrings.

3. Which text message would your dream boyfriend send you?
   a) ❏ hope that u are havin a nice day & that ur guitar lesson goes well. luv u xx
   b) ❏ hey babe, i just drank 2 litres of milk for a dare!!! now i feel sick!!! luv u xx
   c) ❏ Roses are red, violets are blue, sugar is sweet and I will always love you. xx

"Oh no!" Michael said to Laura, as Evie and Samantha were leaving the changing room. "I think I left the football shirt for scene five in the storeroom. But I haven't got any make-up on yet... I haven't got time to get it, Laura – could you?"

changing room	Umkleideraum
storeroom	Lager(raum)
to light	beleuchten
mysterious	geheimnisvoll
to avoid	(ver)meiden
to remain	bleiben
hooded	mit Kapuze, vermummt
to strike	zuschlagen

"No problem, Michael," replied Laura.

"Here are the keys," said Michael. "Just give them back to Mr Adams when you get back."

The drama storeroom was at the other side of the main hall, and Laura had to go outside and walk around the building to get there. It was already dark outside, but, inside the entrance to the hall, Andrew noticed Laura because the schoolyard was well lit by outdoor lights here. I wonder where she's going? he thought to himself, as he stared out of the window. But then he noticed something even stranger. Somebody was following Laura. Somebody, but who?

It was too dark to tell – this mysterious figure was wearing a black coat and hood, and was avoiding the areas lit by outdoor lights. But the figure was definitely following Laura, and was taking great care to remain in the shadows.

"I'll be back in two minutes," Andrew told Alexa Fletcher, who was helping him check tickets.

Then he headed straight outside and began to follow the hooded figure, around the building towards the back entrance, which nobody was using that night.

Laura opened the door and went into the building – the figure followed her seconds later. Andrew took out his mobile and, as quickly as possible, sent Emily a text message:

> come 2 the back entrance of the hall
> now. whoever set u up is about 2
> strike again.

ÜBUNG 24: Prepositions. Vervollständige die Sätze mit den folgenden Präpositionen!

| up | on | at | around | to | in | for | of |

1. Samantha put her coat ....

2. Then she put her hood ....

3. He has left the football shirt .... scene five in the store room.

4. Give the keys .... Mr Adams when you get back.

5. The drama store room was .... the other side .... the main hall.

6. Laura had to walk .... the building to get there.

7. The mysterious figure was taking great care to remain .... the shadows.

True Colours and True Crushes

5

Kurz vor der Premiere von *Seventh Heaven* überschlagen sich die Ereignisse: Während Emily und Holly noch auf dem Weg zu Andrew sind, beobachtet der, wie die vermummte Gestalt Laura ins Theaterlager sperrt. Gleichzeitig versucht Evie, endlich hinter Samanthas Geheimnis zu kommen. Die Freunde setzen alles daran, noch vor Beginn des Stücks den Bösewicht zu überführen und Emilys Unschuld zu beweisen. Und am Ende des Abends ist Emily ihrem ganz eigenen siebten Himmel ein großes Stück näher gekommen …

When Emily received Andrew's text message, more and more people were coming into the hall. She stood up immediately and walked quickly out of the hall.
"Emily!" shouted Alexa, as Emily ran past. "If you see Andrew, tell him to come back – I need some help checking the tickets – we're getting busy!"
But Emily didn't reply – she was already outside, in the schoolyard. While she was running, she took out her mobile phone and rang Evie. But Evie didn't answer, so Emily rang Holly.
Holly answered her phone after only a few seconds. "Hi Emily. What's up?"

"Listen, Holly," said Emily, speaking very quickly. "Something's going on... I think Andrew knows who the culprit is – the person who sent me the threat. Did Samantha confess to Evie, as expected?"

"I don't know – she's not here."

"Okay, Holly, never mind Samantha. You should come and meet me. I might need your help. Meet me at the back entrance to the hall, quickly!"

When Laura was inside the building, she turned the lights on, walked up the stairs, across the hallway and arrived at the drama storeroom. She unlocked the door, turned the light on and went inside. She left the key hanging in the keyhole and began to search for the football shirt.

What's up?	Was ist los?
to unlock	aufschließen
keyhole	Schlüsselloch
to plunge into darkness	in Dunkelheit tauchen

Now, she thought, where could it be? I can't see it anywhere.

Laura didn't hear the door close or the key turn in the keyhole. She only realized that something was wrong when the room plunged into darkness.

"I don't understand why we've come outside, Sammy!" Evie said to Samantha.

The two girls were standing next to the entrance to the main hall. Evie was annoyed because she didn't have the dictaphone with her – it was hidden in her bag in the changing room. If Samantha confesses now I won't have recorded proof, she thought.

"I told you before — We've come outside so that I can tell you my secret and nobody will hear," replied

staircase	Treppe(nhaus)
reflection	Spiegelung, Reflektion
basically	im Grunde, im Prinzip
⚡ to act cool	cool tun
taste	Geschmack

Samantha. "Listen, this is what I wanted to tell you when we were in the café..."

Andrew was standing on the staircase. He saw the hooded figure lock the door, take the keys out and turn off the light.

"Hello!" came a voice from inside the room. "Hello, there's someone in here. Let me out! ... Hello! Hello! Please, open the door — I'm scared on the dark! Hello!"

The hooded figure did not open the door or turn the light back on. When the figure walked up to the window, Andrew saw the window's reflection of the figure's face, like a mirror. The figure smiled at the window and Michael Fernandez's face smiled back.

"Basically, I think Michael's got a huge crush on me," said Samantha to Evie. She was wearing her frog costume and had a green face and green hair. "He flirts so much! But you have to keep it a secret. I don't want people to think I'm bothered. I want to act cool. I want to pretend I'm not

interested at first. But of course I *am*! He's *gorgeous*. Oh Evie, isn't it amazing?"

Evie didn't know what to say. *This* was Samantha's big secret. No enormous confession. Nothing like that. Her big secret was about a crush. And a crush that didn't even exist.

Michael doesn't fancy you! Evie thought. He's got much better taste!

But of course Evie had to lie.

"Oh that's... great news. Fantastic."

"Evie? You don't seem really happy for me... What's wrong? I thought you'd be impressed."

ÜBUNG 25: Who said what? Antworte immer mit einem ganzen Satz!

`Alexa` `Emily` `Holly` `Laura` `Samantha`

1. Who said that Samantha wasn't in the changing room?

   ....

2. Who demanded to be let out?

   ....

3. Who began to tell a secret?

   ....

4. Who asked whether Samantha made a confession?

   ....

5. Who said that lots of people were arriving and therefore she needed some help?

   ....

   ....

"Impressed?!" said Evie. She decided at that moment that the lies had to end. She had lied too much, and it wasn't helping Emily anyway.
"Samantha, I've got to tell you something. Listen, I admit that you can be a laugh. And yes, I enjoyed the milkshake with you on Saturday. But we're not *really* friends, are we? I'm sorry, I haven't been honest with you. Emily is still my best friend. When she got kicked out of the play I was so upset for her. I lied to you because I thought that you might admit that you sent Emily the threat and put Mr Adams' phone in her bag. I'm sorry. I understand if you are angry with me. But I need to ask you one question: Did you do it? Did you get Emily kicked out of the play?"

In the changing room, Mr Adams was beginning to panic.
"Where is Laura Padbury?" he asked Miss Moss. "And Michael Fernandez – where's he? The play is starting in a quarter of an hour – where are they?"
"Don't worry, they'll be here," Miss Moss replied. "They're both very reliable."
"Sir!" cried a couple of girls behind Mr Adams.
It was Bethany Hobson and Nicky Whiteley, the other make-up artists.
"We need help! Evie and Holly have disappeared. We can't do all the make-up on our own!"

to panic	durchdrehen
reliable	zuverlässig

| urgent | dringend |
| firm | sicher, fest |

"What?" said Mr Adams. "More people missing? What on earth is going on? Please, somebody, help Nicky and Bethany with the make-up. I need to..."

Mr Adams was interrupted by Nina. "Sir! I've just got a text message from Emily – Emily Etchells – I think it might answer your question."

Nina read the text message aloud to Mr Adams and Miss Moss. "Tell Mr Adams to come to the drama storeroom immediately – it's urgent."

Mr Adams was not impressed. "Tell Emily Etchells that I have more important things to worry about at the moment!" he shouted.

Miss Moss sighed. "Look, I think this might be important. I'll go."

"I think I should come too, Miss!" said Nina. "In case Emily sends me another message."

And before Mr Adams could stop them, Miss Moss and Nina hurried out of the changing room and headed towards the drama storeroom.

"Let her out!" cried Andrew. "I saw exactly what you did, Michael, now let Laura out!"

Michael was shocked. Oh my God, he thought, It's Andrew Howard! He saw everything!

"Andrew... I never saw you come in... What are you...? Why are you...? Listen, you don't understand."

ÜBUNG 26: True or false? Kreuze die richtigen Aussagen an!

1. Samantha wanted everyone to know how much she liked Michael. ❑

2. Samantha claimed that Michael had a huge crush on her. ❑

3. Evie apologized for lying to Samantha. ❑

4. Mr Adams was not interested in the text message which Nina had received. ❑

5. Nina said that she should go with Miss Moss in case she needs some advice. ❑

"I understand very clearly," Andrew answered, in a firm and confident voice. "You've just locked Laura in the storeroom. Now let her out. *Now*."

"Michael? Michael did this?" came Laura's voice from inside the drama storeroom. "Why, Michael? Please, let me out!"

"Look, Andrew," said Michael. "I did this for... for..." He was taking a long time to choose each word, hesitating as he spoke. Slowly his olive skin turned bright red. "For Emily! Yes, for Emily. I know that Laura threatened her. Laura put Mr Adams' phone in her bag. I promise, it's the truth. Laura did it."

"No, I didn't!" cried Laura. "I didn't! I didn't! Why are you lying, Michael? I don't understand! Your football shirt isn't in here at all, is it? You told me to come here just so that you could lock me in, didn't you? Now let me out! *Please*!"

Laura was beginning to panic. Her voice was shaking and she was beginning to cry. In the darkness tears rolled down her cheeks.

to shake	beben, zittern
tear	Träne
cheek	Wange
⚡ scumbag	Mistkerl
to batter	verprügeln, zusammenschlagen
to grab	greifen, grapschen
to drop sth.	etw. fallen lassen

"You're a lying scumbag," said Andrew. "You might be a good actor, but I can see right through your lies!"

"Oh shut up, you loser," replied Michael. He was quickly realizing that lying wasn't working. "I'm getting out of here. And you can't prove anything."

"But I'll tell the teachers and when they find Laura here, she'll tell them it was you."

"If you mention any of this to the teachers, I'll batter you, I promise. Now, I'm getting out of here."

Michael only had one exit: down the stairs, which meant going past Andrew. As Michael tried to get past him, Andrew pushed Michael against the wall and tried to grab the keys to the storeroom. Michael pushed Andrew onto the floor, just at the top of the stairs, but as he did, Michael dropped the keys.

"Don't you dare say a word," said Michael, and bent down to pick up the keys. But as he stepped around Andrew at the top of the stairs, Andrew managed to stick his leg out into Michael's path. Michael tripped over Andrew's leg and lost his balance. He dropped the keys again and began to fall... and fall... and fall...

"Argh!" he cried as he fell, and his cry echoed around the building and into the schoolyard.

For the first time in a long time, Samantha Lavigne didn't know what to say. Finally she replied, "Do you really think I would threaten your friend? Really? I had no idea that people hated me so much."

Don't you dare!	Wage es ja nicht!
to manage	etw. schaffen
to stick out	hinausstrecken
path	Weg
to trip over sth.	über etw. stolpern
to lose one's balance	das Gleichgewicht verlieren
to echo	widerhallen
agony	Höllenqual

She paused for a few seconds, then continued. "To answer your question: No, I didn't do it. I didn't threaten Emily or put the phone in her bag. And I have no idea who did."

"Okay," Evie replied, "thanks. I believe you."

Suddenly the girls heard Michael's cry. "Argh!"

Without saying a word, they both began to run towards the back entrance of the hall.

Emily and Holly arrived just as Michael had fallen right to the bottom of the stairs and was lying there in agony.

ÜBUNG 27: Verb forms. Vervollständige die Sätze mit der richtigen Zeitform des angegebenen Verbs!

1. Don't worry. They *(be)* .... here before the play starts.

2. We need help! Evie and Holly *(disappear)* ....

3. I did it for Emily. I know that Laura *(threaten)* .... her.

4. Michael *(take)* .... a long time to choose each word.

5. Now, I *(get)* .... out of here.

6. "I *(tell)* .... the teachers," said Andrew.

7. Michael *(lose)* .... his balance and fell down the stairs.

"Michael!" Emily cried. "Oh Michael! Are you alright? What happened? What's going..."
Emily was suddenly distracted from Michael's pain. She noticed something sticking out of the top of his coat pocket. Emily pulled it out. It was a piece of paper, with letters from a newspaper stuck to it.
"Michael... the note... in your pocket... what's going on?"
"Emily!" cried Andrew from the top of the stairs.

He had let Laura out of the storeroom, and now they were both standing at the top of the stairs in shock. Laura's face was damp with sweat and tears, and she was clearly distraught by the whole experience.

stuck to	geklebt an
damp	feucht, klamm
sweat	Schweiß
distraught	bestürzt, außer sich

bone	Knochen
speechless	sprachlos
to sob	schluchzen
fit of tears	Heulanfall

"Emily – that note explains everything! It explains…" But then Andrew was interrupted. "What does it explain?" It was Miss Moss. She had just arrived, with Nina. "What on earth is going on? Michael, are you okay?"

Seconds later, Evie and Samantha also arrived at the scene.
"I can't move!" Michael cried. "It hurts too much! I think I have broken every bone in my body!"
Miss Moss went to help Andrew and noticed the note which Emily was holding.
"Emily… the threat? You were telling the truth, weren't you?"
"Yes, of course I was, Miss," Emily replied.
"Michael sent that note to Emily and locked Laura in the storeroom so that she wouldn't be able to play Jenny," said Andrew.
Emily, Miss Moss and the others stood there, speechless. They were only just realizing exactly what had happened.
"And I suppose you put Mr Adams' phone in Emily's bag too, right? But why, Michael, why?"
"Yes, why, Michael?" sobbed Laura. "I was… I was so scared! I was so scared!" And she burst into a fit of tears.
"For you," came Michael's reply.
Who? thought Emily. Who does he mean, 'you'?
Then Emily realized… Michael was pointing at Samantha.
"I did it all for *you*, Samantha. I want you to play Jenny. I always wanted you to play Jenny!"

"So you locked Laura in the storeroom?!" asked Miss Moss. She was struggling to believe that it was actually true. "And you sent Emily a threat and put Mr Adams' phone in her bag?"

Michael didn't say a word. He just nodded.

"For *me*!" said Samantha, smiling wildly. "You did it all for me?! Oh Michael, I love you! And you love me! I had no idea but... thank you!"

to struggle	sich abmühen
ridiculous	lächerlich
You're welcome to him!	Du kannst ihn haben!
mess	Chaos
barely	kaum
to cut out	rausschneiden

Everyone ignored Samantha's ridiculous comments. You're welcome to him, thought Emily.

"Right," said Miss Moss. "The play needs to start now. We will discuss this mess later. Laura, quickly get ready. But Michael cannot go on stage – he can barely move. Andrew – you'll play Reece tonight."

"But Miss, I can't go on stage, I just can't!" said Laura, still sobbing. "I feel sick... I... I..." She could hardly talk because she was crying so much.

"But we need a Jenny!" Miss Moss cried. "Samantha – you are the understudy, you'll be Jenny. We'll cut the frog out of the play, that's not a problem."

"I'd love to, Miss! After all, Michael did all of this for *me*... But have you seen the colour of my hair? I'm completely green! Jenny can't have green hair!" Samantha replied.

"Well, what about Emily?" Nina suggested. "She knows the part. She's been practising it for weeks. And besides, now we have proof that she isn't a thief."

"Emily... would you? Would you play Jenny?" asked Miss Moss.

"Really?" asked Emily. "Are you really asking me to play Jenny?"

"Yes!" Miss Moss answered. "Yes, of course!"

"Then quick!" Emily said. "I've got to get into costume!"

to come to an end	enden, aufhören
to rush	eilen, hetzen
thrilled	begeistert, erregt
to make it	es schaffen

An hour and a half later, the first performance of the play was coming to an end. Of course, the audience was filled with families and friends: Nina's, Holly's and Evie's parents were there, as well as Evie's brothers Olly, Simon and Max, Holly's older sister Sophie and Nina's younger sister Katja.

Mr and Mrs Etchells were also there – they'd rushed to the school as quickly as possible when Emily told them that she would be playing Jenny after all. Holly and Evie also sat in the hall, amazed but thrilled that Emily was acting on stage in front of them.

"Finally we have made it, Reece," Emily said to Andrew. *"Finally, the troubles have passed, and you are still here. This time I know that I'll never lose you again. Finally, we are in our very own seventh heaven."*

ÜBUNG 28: Reading comprehension. Beantworte die folgenden Fragen!

1. Why was Emily suddenly distracted from Michael's pain?

....

2. Who did Miss Moss interrupt when she arrived with Nina?

....

3. Michael says that he locked Laura in the cupboard for one particular person – who?

....

4. Why does Laura not want to play Jenny?

....

5. Why can't Samantha play Jenny?

....

"I love you, Jenny," Andrew replied. *"Without you, my life would be nothing at all. But you know, baby, this is just the beginning. We've reached our seventh heaven but the best is still to come."*

There was a short pause, then the audience began to applaud, and applaud and applaud. The play was an enormous success. As the actors came to bow, the audience rose to their feet. A standing ovation!

Everyone had worked so hard for this moment – but nobody had worked harder than Emily.

to applaud	klatschen
to bow	sich verbeugen
to rise (to one's feet)	sich erheben, aufstehen
to be fooled	getäuscht werden
to trick	betrügen, hereinlegen
to brainwash sb.	bei jmd. eine Gehirnwäsche vornehmen
to get rid of sb.	jmd. loswerden

This is my seventh heaven, Emily thought, and my best friends and I worked for every second of it.

"Emily! Nina! You were amazing!" cried Holly, as she and Evie came into the changing room after the show.

"And don't forget Andrew," said Evie. "You made a fantastic Reece – it should have been you from the start."

Andrew turned red; he was not used to such compliments from girls.

"And thank you, all of you," said Emily, "for always being there for me when everybody else thought that I was a thief and a liar. I was so stupid to be fooled by Michael's false charm. He tricked me, lied to me and completely brainwashed me. But you were there all along. Thank you. You're the best friends anyone could ever have."

"You're welcome Emily," said Nina. "We're only so nice because you're a super friend, too! But what a huge surprise – I never suspected Michael! I can't believe I had a crush on someone who would do something so awful! What a huge mistake that was."

"I know," said Holly. "He seemed so nice. But really he wanted to get rid of you *and* Laura, so that Samantha could play Jenny. Do you think Samantha knew? Is that what she wanted to tell you, Evie?"

ÜBUNG 29: *Match-up. Welche Wörter passen inhaltlich zusammen?*

1. first
2. younger
3. costume
4. seventh
5. enormous
6. standing
7. best

heaven
friends
performance
success
ovation
sister
designing

"No, we were completely wrong for suspecting Samantha," Evie replied. "She didn't have a clue about Michael's plan. But she did suspect that Michael fancied her – that was her big secret."

"Really?" asked Emily. "You know, I never expected him to fancy her. But now we know his true colours, I expect they'll be happy together!"

"Definitely!" agreed Nina. "They'll be the most bitchy, self-centred couple in the whole school!"

They all laughed at this. Then, when they had gathered all of their things, they began to make their way out of the changing room.

"But I still can't believe it's true," said Emily, "that I did play Jenny, after everything that happened. It still feels a bit like a dream."

"Yeah, me too," said Andrew. "I never expected things to turn out so... perfectly." He smiled at Emily. It was the same nervous smile that he had given her weeks ago, on her doorstep. Back then, Emily had ignored his smile when her mum appeared. But not this time.

⚡ to not have a clue	keine Ahnung haben
true colours	wahres Gesicht
⚡ bitchy	gemein, zickig
self-centred	egozentrisch
to gather	einsammeln
to turn out	ausgehen, ausfallen
to hint at	auf etw. hindeuten
just right	genau richtig

Emily smiled back, and this time the smile hinted at something slightly more than friendship.

"I know," she replied. "Things really have turned out perfectly."

"Oh my..." Holly began to say, but then Evie gave her a look which said 'don't say a word.'

Evie, Holly and Nina were all thinking the same thing: Emily might have finally found somebody just right.

The best thing of all, however, was that Emily was also thinking this very thing: At last, I might have found somebody just right.

ÜBUNG 30: Can your friends count on you? Finde heraus, ob deine Freundinnen wirklich auf dich zählen können!

1. You are at the cinema with your boyfriend. You get this text message from your best friend: I'm so upset. Danny and I have split up. What do you do?
   a) ❏ You leave the cinema immediately, go to your friend's house and comfort her.
   b) ❏ You reply: I'll ring you when the film has finished. After the film you call her.
   c) ❏ You ignore the message and think she'll be alright.

2. It is your best friend's birthday, but you don't have any money to buy her a present. So you...
   a) ❏ borrow £30 from your parents to buy her an expensive present.
   b) ❏ make her a photo album with nice photos of you both.
   c) ❏ don't bother to get her a present – she only spent a couple of pounds on you, after all!

3. You have got a ticket to see your best friend in the school play, but you feel really ill. You...
   a) ❏ go to the play anyway to support her.
   b) ❏ stay in bed and send your friend a good luck text message.
   c) ❏ stay in bed and even using a mobile phone is too much effort!

Lösungen

ÜBUNG 1:

1. to play the guitar 2. to audition for a play 3. to wear trendy designer clothes 4. to love somebody's smile 5. to walk to school 6. to listen to rock bands 7. to style your hair

ÜBUNG 2:

1. richtig 2. falsch (Emily thought the auditions for the part of Reece were the previous day.) 3. richtig 4. falsch (Emily did understand when Nina wrote "Ich liebe Michael" on her pencil case.) 5. falsch (Samantha has less acting ability than Laura.)

ÜBUNG 3:

1	2	3	4	5	6	7
e	b	f	a	g	c	d

ÜBUNG 4:

1. r 2. x 3. plz 4. rly 5. c u soon 6. bday 7. txt bk 8. 4 9. prob 10. 2 11. luv 12. wer

ÜBUNG 5:

1. b 2. c 3. c 4. b

ÜBUNG 6:

1. Evie says that she has to see a teacher.
2. Holly asks Emily if she had a nice weekend.
3. Emily explains that she's just so forgetful.
4. Nina asks Emily to finish her sentence.
5. Emily says that she has been thinking about *Seventh Heaven* a lot lately.

6. Nina says that Emily should talk to Evie.
7. Emily thinks that the situation is very frustrating.

ÜBUNG 7:

1. hilarious 2. brilliant 3. surprised 4. ponytail
5. reaction 6. enormous

ÜBUNG 8:

Mostly a): You would get on with Samantha – because just like her, you think you are the best person in the world and everyone else is either ugly, weird or both.

Mostly b): You would get on with Emily and Holly – because just like them, you live in a world of daydreams and romance.

Mostly c): You would get on with Laura – because just like her, you love drama but you are timid so you would only dare to speak to each other!

Mostly d): You would get on with Nina and Evie – because like them, you are outgoing and like keeping busy, which includes meeting lots of new people.

ÜBUNG 9:

1. Keep quiet or I'll blow up your locker.
2. Leave town, or we'll tell everyone your dirty secret.
3. Stay away from my boyfriend, or I'll steal yours.
4. Give us £20, or we'll never speak to you again.
5. Show me that text message, or I'll throw your bag in the river.

ÜBUNG 10:

Horizontal: evil, kind, selfish, stubborn

Vertikal: unfriendly, daring, confident

Diagonal: amazing, independent, annoying

ÜBUNG 11:
1. here 2. wants 3. go 4. receive 5. darling 6. quickly 7. living room

ÜBUNG 12:
1. falsch (It was Nina's phone.) 2. richtig 3. richtig 4. richtig 5. falsch (The bell rang before the girls got outside.) 6. richtig

ÜBUNG 13:
1. for 2. in 3. with 4. into 5. onto 6. to 7. amongst

ÜBUNG 14:
1. At lunchtime Emily was talking to Andrew.
2. Nina's playing Emma-Jayne Maynard.
3. Michael's voice is described as sexy and smooth.
4. He thinks that Emily is a different person when Michael is around.
5. Emily believes that Nina is threatening her because she saw a piece of newspaper in her bag.
6. No, Andrew thinks that Samantha is threatening Emily.

ÜBUNG 15:
Mostly a): Do not share your secret with this boy! He will pretend to listen and that he cares, but really he just wants to tell the school which will humiliate you.

Mostly b): It is difficult to know if you should share your secret or not. Only tell him if it is for the right reasons (because you have a genuine problem… NOT because you think it will make him notice you)!

Mostly c): You can definitely tell him – He is Mr Kind, Considerate and Caring, and he would not share your secret with anyone.

ÜBUNG 16:
1. were playing 2. took 3. noticed 4. meets 5. felt 6. need

ÜBUNG 17:

1	2	3	4	5	6
c	f	a	e	b	d

ÜBUNG 18:

1. everyone 2. any 3. top 4. anyone 5. everything 6. with

ÜBUNG 19:

```
 N E W S P A P E R
   M     E       P
   B   B R I L L I A N T
 B A G   F       G
   R   W O R L D E
   R     R       B
   A     M       I
   S     A       R
   S   I N N O C E N T
   M     C       H
 Y E S T E R D A Y D
   N             A
 S T A G E       Y
```

ÜBUNG 20:

1. play 2. was 3. had 4. gained 5. put 6. are 7. saying

ÜBUNG 21:

1. b 2. c 3. c 4. a

ÜBUNG 22:

1. quickly 2. anxiety 3. character 4. audience 5. accident

ÜBUNG 23:

Mostly a): Your dream boyfriend is Andrew. He may not have a lot of money to spend on expensive presents, but he is thoughtful, kind and affectionate.

Mostly b): Your dream boyfriend is Owen. He doesn't like romance – he just wants to have a laugh with you!

Mostly c): Your dream boyfriend is Michael. You often receive red roses and other romantic gifts from him – he is the definition of ROMANCE!

ÜBUNG 24:

1. on 2. up 3. for 4. to 5. at, of 6. around 7. in

ÜBUNG 25:

1. Holly said that Samantha wasn't in the changing room.
2. Laura demanded to be let out.
3. Samantha began to tell a secret.
4. Emily asked whether Samantha made a confession.
5. Alexa said that lots of people were arriving and therefore she needed some help.

ÜBUNG 26:

1. falsch (Samantha said that she didn't want people to think she was bothered.)
2. richtig
3. richtig
4. richtig
5. falsch (Nina said that she should go with Miss Moss in case Emily sent her another text message.)

ÜBUNG 27:

1. will be 2. have disappeared 3. threatened 4. was taking 5. am getting 6. will tell 7. lost

ÜBUNG 28:

1. She noticed the note in Michael's coat pocket.
2. Miss Moss interrupted Andrew.

3. He did it for Samantha.
4. She feels sick.
5. Her hair is completely green, and Jenny can't have green hair!

ÜBUNG 29:

1. first performance 2. younger sister
3. costume designing 4. seventh heaven
5. enormous success 6. standing ovation
7. best friends

ÜBUNG 30:

Mostly a): You're a super friend! Your friend can count on you for anything. However, be careful, because sometimes being too nice can lead to problems for your purse and your health!

Mostly b): Your friend can definitely rely on you, but you also realize that it is important to look after other people besides your best friend: your family, your boyfriend and yourself.

Mostly c): Oh no! You don't think about your best friend's happiness much. You seriously need to become more reliable; otherwise soon you won't have a best friend at all.

Glossar

to accuse	anklagen
achievement	Leistung
act	Theater, Show
⚡ to act cool	cool tun
actor	Schauspieler
actress	Schauspielerin
actual(ly)	eigentlich, tatsächlich
to add up	einen Sinn ergeben
to admit	zugeben
affection	Zuneigung
agony	Höllenqual
alarmed	alarmiert, beunruhigt
alongside	Seite an Seite mit, neben
amazing	super, erstaunlich
ambitious	ehrgeizig
announcements page	Anzeigenseite
annoyed	verärgert
annoying	ärgerlich
answer-phone	Anrufbeantworter
anxiety	Angst, Unruhe
to apologize	sich entschuldigen
to appear	erscheinen
to applaud	klatschen
to arrange to meet	sich verabreden
attention-seeker	jmd., der die Beachtung von anderen sucht
audience	Publikum
audition	Vorsprechen
to audition	vorsprechen
to avoid	(ver)meiden
awkwardly	ungeschickt

backstage	hinter der Bühne
baggy	schlabberig, sackartig
barely	kaum
basically	im Grunde, im Prinzip
to batter	verprügeln, zusammenschlagen
to be fooled	getäuscht werden
to beg	betteln
to be mad at sb.	auf jmd. wütend sein
besides	außerdem
⚡ bitchy	gemein, zickig
bitter	verbittert
to blush	erröten
bone	Knochen
⚡ to bop around	herumspringen
to bother	stören
to bow	sich verbeugen
to brainwash sb.	bei jmd. eine Gehirnwäsche vornehmen
briefcase	Aktentasche
bully	Raufbold
to bump into sth.	mit etw. zusammenstoßen
to burst out laughing	in Gelächter ausbrechen
canteen	Kantine
capable of	fähig zu
carelessly	sorglos
caretaker	Hausmeister
cast	Ensemble
certainly	zweifellos
changing room	Umkleideraum
to chat	sich unterhalten, plaudern
cheek	Wange
to cheer	jauchzen, jubeln
⚡ chitchat	Geplauder
co-director	Mitregisseur(in)
to come to an end	enden, aufhören
completely shocked	total bestürzt
to concentrate	sich konzentrieren

to confess	gestehen
confident	selbstbewusst
to congratulate	gratulieren
Congratulations!	Glückwunsch!
to consider sth.	etw. beachten, an etw. denken
costume designer	Kostümbildner(in)
covered in	verschmiert mit
crew	Team
culprit	Täter(in), Schuldige(r)
curiously	neugierig
to cut (cut, cut) out	rausschneiden
damp	feucht, klamm
dare	*hier:* Wette
daring	wagemutig
daydream	Tagtraum
deaf	taub
deliberately	mit Absicht
to deny	bestreiten
to deserve	verdienen
desperately	unbedingt
devastated	am Boden zerstört
dictaphone	Diktiergerät
disinterested	desinteressiert
distant	fern, weit weg
to distract	ablenken
distraught	bestürzt, außer sich
Don't you dare!	Wage es ja nicht!
to drop sth.	etw. fallen lassen
to dye (dyed, dyed)	färben
to echo	widerhallen
embarrassment	Verlegenheit
emotion	Gefühl
envelope	Briefumschlag
evidence	Beweis
excitement	Aufregung
to expect	erwarten
fabric	Stoff

fake	unecht
to fall for sb.	sich in jmd. verknallen
false	unecht
⚡ to fancy sb.	auf jmd. stehen
to feel (felt, felt) down	niedergeschlagen sein
firm	sicher, fest
fit of tears	Heulanfall
to fold one's arms	die Arme verschränken
for some reason	aus irgendeinem Grund
to gain	erlangen, gewinnen
to gather	einsammeln
genuinely	echt
gesture	Geste
⚡ to get (got, got) it	etw. verstehen
to get oneself into hot water	in Teufels Küche kommen
to get (got, got) on with sb.	mit jmd. auskommen
to get rid of sb.	jmd. loswerden
giddily	benommen vor Aufregung
to glare at	anstarren
to go (went, gone) out with sb.	mit jmd. (aus)gehen
gorgeous	wunderschön, großartig
to grab	greifen, grapschen
guilt	Schuld
⚡ to hang (hung, hung) out	abhängen
⚡ to have a crush on sb.	in jmd. verknallt sein
to have sth. on one's mind	etw. im Sinn haben
headlines	Schlagzeilen
to head to(wards)	zusteuern auf
He didn't mind.	Es war ihm egal.
to hesitate	zögern
hilarious	wahnsinnig komisch
to hint at	auf etw. hindeuten
⚡ hiya	hey, hallo
hood	Kapuze
hooded	mit Kapuze, vermummt
to hug	(sich) umarmen
huge	riesig
to hurry	eilen

123

I can't wait.	Ich freue mich darauf.
ice-cream parlour	Eisdiele
impressed	beeindruckt
indeed	tatsächlich
to indicate	(an)zeigen
in private	unter vier Augen
to interrupt	unterbrechen
I told you so.	Ich hab's dir doch gesagt.
jealous	eifersüchtig
joker	Spaßvogel
just right	genau richtig
to keep a secret	ein Geheimnis bewahren
to keep one's promises	seine Versprechen halten
keyhole	Schlüsselloch
⚡ to kick out	rausschmeißen
lad	Kumpel, Junge
let's get started	lasst uns loslegen
liar	Lügner(in)
to light (lit, lit)	beleuchten
lighting	Beleuchtung
locker	Schließfach
to lose one's balance	das Gleichgewicht verlieren
main female character	weibliche Hauptfigur
to make (made, made) it	es schaffen
to make one's way	gehen, sich begeben
to manage	etw. schaffen
⚡ mate	Kumpel
meanwhile	mittlerweile
to memorize	auswendig lernen
to mention	erwähnen
mess	Chaos
monologue	Monolog
⚡ moron	Trottel
motive	Motiv, Beweggrund
Mr Popular	jmd., der sehr beliebt ist
⚡ Must dash!	Ich muss los!
mysterious	geheimnisvoll
nasty	gemein

nerves	Nervosität
never mind	macht nichts, mach dir nichts daraus
nevertheless	trotzdem, nichtsdestoweniger
newsagent's	Zeitungskiosk
newsreader	Nachrichtensprecher
to nod	nicken
⚡ to not have a clue	keine Ahnung haben
No way!	Auf keinen Fall!
obvious	offensichtlich
odd	merkwürdig, seltsam
on purpose	mit Absicht
to over-react	überreagieren
to panic	durchdrehen
part	Rolle
particular	bestimmt
path	Weg
pathetic	erbärmlich
performance	Aufführung, Darbietung
plain	gewöhnlich
⚡ to play dirty	unfaire Mittel anwenden
to pluck up the courage to do sth.	sich ein Herz fassen, etw. zu tun
to plunge into darkness	in Dunkelheit tauchen
to pretend	so tun, als ob
prime suspect	Hauptverdächtige(r)
proof	Beweis
properly	richtig
to prove	beweisen
to quit (quit, quit)	aufhören mit, aufgeben
ransom note	Erpresserbrief
rational	vernünftig
to react	reagieren
to realize	bemerken, begreifen
reassuringly	beruhigend
to record	aufzeichnen
reflection	Spiegelung, Reflektion

to refuse	ablehnen, sich weigern
registration	Anwesenheitskontrolle
rehearsal	Probe
reliable	zuverlässig
reluctantly	widerstrebend
to remain	bleiben
to remark	bemerken, anmerken
to reply	antworten
to require	erfordern, voraussetzen
ridiculous	lächerlich
ring-tone	Klingelton
to rise (to one's feet)	sich erheben, aufstehen
root	Wurzel
to rush	eilen, hetzen
sb.'s heart sinks	jmd. rutscht das Herz in die Hose
scenery	Kulisse
school play	Schultheaterstück
script	Skript (des Stücks)
⚡ scumbag	Mistkerl
secretly	heimlich
self-centred	egozentrisch
selfish	egoistisch
sensation	Gefühl
sensitively	einfühlsam
set	Set, Bühnenbild
to set sb. up	hereinlegen
to sew (sewed, sewn)	nähen
to shake (shook, shaken)	beben, zittern
⚡ She was rubbish.	Sie war grottenschlecht.
shy	schüchtern
to sigh	seufzen
slightly confused	ein bisschen verwirrt
to slip away	weggleiten, schwinden
slyly	listig
smooth	glatt, weich
to sob	schluchzen
to solve	lösen (Problem)

sound	Ton
speechless	sprachlos
to spin (spun, spun)	sich drehen
to split (split, split) up	(sich) trennen
spot	Pickel
staircase	Treppe(nhaus)
to step down	zurücktreten
to stick by sb.	zu jmd. halten
to stick (stuck, stuck) out	herausragen, hinausstrecken
storeroom	Lager(raum)
straight away	sofort, unverzüglich
strict	streng
to strike (struck, struck)	zuschlagen
to struggle	sich abmühen
stubborn	stur
stuck to	geklebt an
stunningly	erstaunlich
stylish	modisch, stylish
suited	passend, geeignet
to suspect	den Verdacht haben, dass
suspicion	Verdacht, Verdächtigung
suspicious	misstrauisch, argwöhnisch
sweat	Schweiß
to tap	tippen, klopfen
taste	Geschmack
tear	Träne
text message	SMS
That's good of you.	Das ist nett von dir.
there was real chemistry	die Chemie stimmte
thief	Dieb(in)
threat	Drohung
to threaten	bedrohen
thrilled	begeistert, erregt
tied tightly	fest gebunden
to trick	betrügen, hereinlegen
to trip over sth.	über etw. stolpern
true colours	wahres Gesicht
to trust sb.	jmd. vertrauen

to turn out	ausgehen, ausfallen
two-faced	heuchlerisch
unconvincingly	wenig überzeugend
understanding	verständnisvoll
understudy	Zweitbesetzung
unless	wenn nicht, falls nicht
to unlock	aufschließen
urgent	dringend
vicious	bösartig, gemein
victim	Opfer
villain	Bösewicht
⚡ weirdo	Spinner
⚡ What are you up to?	Was hast du vor?
what on earth	was zum Teufel
What's up?	Was ist los?
to whisper	flüstern
wise	klug
to work	*hier:* funktionieren
You're welcome to him!	Du kannst ihn haben!